Goddesses

Goddesses

LANIER GRAHAM

A TINY FOLIO™
ABBEVILLE PRESS   PUBLISHERS
NEW YORK   LONDON   PARIS

To my mother, Martha, and my daughter, Jennifer

CONTENTS

Introduction

Until the late twentieth century there was little one could read about goddesses. They were not considered important, either historically or spiritually, by many people in the urbanized West. If thought about at all, goddesses were usually dismissed as a curious aspect of Asian and tribal traditions, which had not played a significant part in Western culture since the days of ancient Greece and Rome. Anyone wanting to read about a goddess had to consult an encyclopedia of religion or mythology for short entries or select from a few books by a handful of anthropologists, classicists, and mythologists.

Until about twenty years ago there was very little awareness of the power and cross-cultural universality of goddess worship in preurbanized Europe. The evidence was slight, and the interest of the male-oriented scholarly establishment was even slighter. But in the middle of the 1970s a paradigm shift took place, partly inspired by the rapid development of the women's movement. A number of books appeared that revolutionized how people looked at the roots of their spiritual heritage. Among the most influential were *The Goddesses and Gods of Old Europe* (1974) by Marija Gimbutas, an archaeologist, and *When God Was a Woman* (1976) by Merlin Stone, an art historian. Although there are some errors in these books, and although some of the language in Gimbutas's book is not the language of critical analysis, the visual evidence they presented was impressive.

Not only did the European ancestors of the modern civilized world believe in goddesses as much as in gods, but the Great Goddess sometimes appears to have been more important than the Great God. History textbooks had been stating or implying that the male had always been dominant in Western theology. Now there were solid arguments for a very different view of the theology of prehistoric Europe—the theory that until the male-dominated Indo-Europeans invaded much of Old Europe, the position there of the Great Goddess had been at least equal to that of the Great God and sometimes probably superior. The combination of traditional evidence from the archaeology and mythology of places such as Crete with evidence newly excavated from southeastern Europe sent shock waves through the academic establishment. When Riane Eisler's book *The Chalice and the Blade* appeared in 1987, providing an overview of all these new findings and their implications, it was hailed by Ashley Montagu, one of the world's leading anthropologists, as the "most important book since Darwin's *Origin of the Species.*"

Western culture had been dominated by the male-oriented values of Indo-European culture for so long that it took a social revolution—the women's movement—to start to bring it into balance. The women's movement in the early 1970s did not begin with specifically female images of divinity as ideals. But once the books by Gimbutas, Stone, and others provided powerful inspiration, the fight for equality expanded beyond the social, political, and economic into the realm of the sacred. As the consciousness movement expanded during the 1970s and started to integrate the spiritual traditions of East and West, men as well as women began to realize that throughout most of human history divinities had been male and female. There had been shamans and shamanesses of equal power. There had been priests and priestesses with equal respect and authority.

The evidence from archaeology, mythology, and linguistics indicates that goddess cultures tended to be egalitarian, earth-centered, and nonviolent. The image of the earth as sacred and of society as balanced between male and female has become a powerful inspiration to people in the women's movement, the ecology movement, the consciousness movement, the goddess movement, and many other new ways of thinking. The ideal of a male-female balance has been articulated more clearly each decade in psychology, sociology, and theology. A more balanced perspective on the cultural history of Europe and the rest of the world is now being taught in Western colleges and universities—no small change.

If the goddess had been so important for most of human history, why did she disappear in the West? The reasons are complex, but one of the most important is that a few thousand years ago many goddess-oriented civilizations were destroyed by extremely aggressive Indo-European tribes. They demolished the old cities and then reconfigured civilization throughout most of the settled world from Greece to India. These barbarians worshiped aggressive sky gods and had scant room in their theology for goddesses; to them, women were little more than property and sexual objects. Not only did male gods become supreme, but females lost their sacredness, in a dramatic turning-around in human history that my friend Joseph Campbell called the "patriarchal inversion." It was even argued by some fathers of the early Christian Church in Rome that women had no souls. Twentieth-century men have at last started to realize that when males lost their reverence for that which is female, they also lost something within themselves.

The goddess, in numerous manifestations, still plays a central role in Taoism and Hinduism, which are the oldest of the great world religions of today. Together with Buddhism, these polytheistic religions have been described collectively as "religions of the earth." Their roots go back tens of thousands of years. They have never severed their connectedness with the primordial reality of Mother

Earth, the Great Goddess whose body is the earth. The Great Goddess, as well as many other goddesses, has always been central to these earth-oriented traditions.

The newer of the great world religions—Judaism, Christianity, and Islam—have been described collectively as "religions of the sky." These religions took shape not during the Stone or the Bronze Age but during the Iron Age, when men dominated the societies of Europe and the Near East. These three religions are monotheistic. In their view, there is only one God, and he is male. There are female saints and angels with female qualities, but there are no Judaic, Christian, or Islamic goddesses that are worshiped as divine in their own right instead of as aspects of God. The Great Goddess was there at the beginning of these three spiritual traditions, but then she disappeared.

The Goddess in the Old Stone Age

Cultural historians divide early human history into the Old Stone Age (the Paleolithic), the New Stone Age (the Neolithic), the Bronze Age, and the Iron Age. The Stone Age world was tribal, even after agriculture appeared about ten thousand years ago, marking the transition from Paleolithic to Neolithic. When villages evolved into the first cities—during the Bronze Age, beginning about five thousand years ago—society still remained semitribal. Not until the Iron Age, from about three thousand years ago, were the collective values of tribal people gradually replaced by the individual values of literate, urbanized people. The Great Goddess was central to the minds and hearts of all Stone Age people, and still is throughout the tribal world, from the Aborigines of Australia to the Kung of Africa.

How long was the Great Goddess central to the society and theology of our ancestors? How long is human history? The answer is uncertain. Scientists and Creationists will be debating this question for some time. Anthropologists have theories that go back millions of years, but their evidence is slim. In terms of clear physical proof, the continuous record of human life on earth starts about one hundred thousand years ago. This date can be used to mark the beginning of the Old Stone Age.

Old Stone Age culture centered on hunting, on gathering food, and on sacred ceremonies. Then, and now, Old Stone Age people lived in small groups that would move from place to place following the movements of the animals that sustained them. Tools, clothing, and shelters were made of stone, hides, bone, and other natural materials. Stone tools were particularly important, hence the name Stone Age. Toward the end of the Old Stone Age, about thirty thousand to twenty thousand years ago, were produced the first known works of art, including cave paintings of astonishing power and many forms of small sculpture. The best-known examples have been found in Europe, between the Atlantic and Russia, but there are parallel examples from every inhabited continent. Art obviously was central to life in the Old Stone Age. Those who think of such art as mere leisure-time activity do not understand tribal culture. Tribal art is sacred art.

Moreover, those works of art are intimately related to the Great Goddess. We can never know all the exact details; however, very similar art is still being made today by people whose culture probably has changed little in the past twenty or thirty thousand years. They have shared much of the meaning of their art with modern anthropologists. To tribal people, there is no separate domain called "religion"; all life is sacred. Tribal people depend on animals not only for food but also as totemic ancestors and highly supportive spiritual guardians who sacrifice themselves in the hunt so that the life of the tribe can continue. When young people are initiated into the wisdom of the tribe, they come to feel at one with their own animal nature and with the sacred totality of the universe.

The subject matter of Paleolithic art consists mainly of animals, with some female figurines that probably represent the Great Goddess, who is the Mother of All. She is the source of all the plants, animals, people, and stars. It is from her body that all the world issues, and everything returns to her body at the end of its time. In one aspect, she is beautiful, all-loving and all-giving. In another aspect, she is terrifying, taking back everything at the time of death. It is nature's endless cycle of birth, death, and rebirth. Many rituals are conducted to ensure that she will continue to give birth to all that is. This probably is why cave paintings were made deep inside the earth, which was (and is) thought of as her body. Inside such Paleolithic "cathedrals," the shamans and shamanesses likely conducted rituals of fertility, hunting, and initiation.

The typical Old Stone Age figurine of the Great Goddess is sculpted to emphasize fertility. She often appears to be pregnant, with huge breasts full of milk, as in the famous *Goddess of Willendorf* (opposite). That figure also is typical in that the body is naturalistic but the head is not. This is probably not a portrait of a person but a representation of that universal being we call the Great Goddess. Figures of this general type continued to be made in the New Stone Age and the Bronze Age. Sometimes they are simple clay shapes. Sometimes they are of stone or ivory or marble. Sometimes they have a long, phallic neck and head, which probably symbolizes the idea that the Great Goddess is both female and male, with the power to create the world all alone. No male is required.

Goddess of Willendorf. Old Stone Age, c. 30,000–20,000 B.C.E.
Red ocher on limestone, height: 4⅜ in. (11 cm).
Naturhistorisches Museum, Vienna.

The Goddess in the New Stone Age

New Stone Age culture centered on agriculture and animal husbandry, which gradually replaced hunting and gathering. The discovery of agriculture (probably by women) about ten thousand years ago revolutionized social patterns. Wandering tribes settled down in villages. Because agriculture can feed many more people than hunting can, villages eventually grew into towns. Neolithic people also developed pottery, weaving, and stone tools that they not only chipped but polished. This way of life is still being lived by about 100 million tribal people in the nonurban areas of Africa, Australia, Asia, Oceania, and the Americas, who continue to think of all matter as pervaded with spirit. With these socioeconomic changes came changes in theology. As in the Old Stone Age, the world of the New Stone Age was filled with gods and goddesses who personified various forces and conditions in the natural world.

Creation myths tell us much about the value system of any society. Creation myths of the Old Stone Age tend to feature the Great Goddess alone; creation myths of the New Stone Age usually give the Great Goddess a partner. How powerful the male is in the myth usually reflects how powerful males are in that society. The partner named first in the myth usually is considered more powerful. Often it is the Great Goddess's son who becomes her lover and thus the father of the world. The words in the myths and the images in the art often show this god as a figure of lesser importance.

Sometimes the Great Goddess and the Great God are regarded as equal. A typical creation myth of this type has the world being created by Brother Sun and Sister Moon; in other cases, the progenitors are animals. Quite frequently the supreme couple is Mother Earth and Father Sky. One of the most important ceremonies of the year is the Sacred Marriage of the earth goddess and the sky god during the new year's ritual, in which a high priestess and a high priest (dressed in shamanic animal hides) personify the supreme deities. In the nonlinear mindset of tribal people, the creation of the universe did not happen just once; it happens again every year. The shamanic Sacred Marriage ritual ensures that the world will be born again and again and again.

Much art of the New Stone Age type is focused on the cosmic relationship of the Great Goddess with the Great God, but there are also many images devoted to other goddesses (or other aspects of the Great Goddess, depending on one's perspective). The more complex the culture, the more specialized the roles of the goddess. In less complex societies, many goddesses have no proper names; they are thought of, for example, as the Earth Spirit or Grandmother Growth. In more complex societies, and in all literate societies, goddesses have proper names, such as Demeter or Ceres.

The linear mindset of literate, urbanized people insists on neat, clear distinctions, such as "this goddess is the goddess of the river, not the stream." However, much melts together in the tribal mind. One goddess can have many aspects, and goddesses often are conceptualized as aspects of the Great Goddess. We in the late twentieth century might be confused by the fact that Athena, the protector of Athens, was both a wisdom goddess and a war goddess; but the Greeks of the Stone Age, the Bronze Age, and the Iron Age were not confused by this.

The Goddess in the Bronze Age

The Bronze Age got its name because it was then that people learned how to make bronze, which became an important medium for weapons and for works of art. The people of the Bronze Age created much more than bronze, however; they created civilization. Civilization is defined in different ways, but most specialists would agree that the essential characteristics of a civilized society (usually with a population of at least ten thousand people) are a written language, monumental architecture, and large-scale sculpture. These elements appeared together for the first time in Mesopotamia and Egypt between five thousand and six thousand years ago; later, they developed elsewhere—most notably, in Crete, Greece, India, China, and Mesoamerica.

The social structure appears to have been quite similar in all these civilizations. The primary economy was agriculture on a scale so large that it had to be managed by special administrators, usually a semishamanic priestly class who could read and write. That they were highly intelligent is obvious from what they designed and caused to be executed: not only brilliant ideographic languages but also astonishing paintings, sculpture, and architecture—including astronomical observatories, beautiful temples, and remarkable sacred pyramids of various shapes and sizes in Mesopotamia, Egypt, India, China, and the Americas.

Society was still semitribal in the Bronze Age. As a rule, at the top of the social structure was a priest-king or a priestess-queen, who was regarded as divine—human embodiments of the Great Goddess and the Great God. The theology continued to be animistic and polytheistic. The clans continued to identify with totemic animals. From Egypt to Mesoamerica, murals show the royalty and the nobility dressed in the same kind of totemic animal hides that their Stone Age ancestors had worn. Their written prayers resemble the Stone Age oral prayers that are still in use today.

Bronze Age goddesses and gods were portrayed in a manner halfway between the Stone Age and Iron Age modes. One rarely sees a human shape in a Stone Age painting; divine animals and an occasional shaman dressed as an animal are the primary subjects. In Bronze Age art, divinities are frequently portrayed as part animal and part human. The most familiar examples are the Sphinx of Egypt and the Minotaur of Crete. Not until the Iron Age were most divinities commonly portrayed as entirely human. The totemic double images either disappeared or were reduced and restructured as animal associates—creatures known in the shamanic world as "power animals" or "spirit allies."

The art and mythology of the Bronze Age are filled with an extraordinary variety of goddesses and gods. The primary divinities of the creation myths tended to remain as they were in the New Stone Age—a partnership of female and male, most often earth and sky. The Sacred Marriage of earth and sky was celebrated regularly in the most holy of temples. Life itself depended on this ritual.

The type of writing that first appeared in the New Stone Age is called pictographic, in which ideas are represented by pictures. Bronze Age writing is ideographic, in which objects and beings are represented by pictures. This kind of writing is halfway toward the alphabetic writing of the Iron Age. Scholars have learned to read most of the ideographic writing of Egypt, Mesopotamia, and China, and much of the writing of Mesoamerica, but the writing

Figurine of a Goddess. Central Anatolia, early Bronze
Age, c. 2500–2000 B.C.E. Silver with gold inlays and
gold leaf boots, height: 4¼ in. (10.8 cm). Museum of Fine Arts,
Boston; Anonymous gift in memory of James Bishop Peabody.

of Minoan Crete and of India remains a mystery. Enough is known that we now have names for many of the goddesses and gods of the Bronze Age as well as a fairly good idea of their attributes. While the names and faces differ from culture to culture, the general pattern is similar worldwide: For every human need, there is a goddess or a god to call upon, be it for life, love, victory, rain, or the relief of pain. Every event in the natural world has a supernatural explanation.

At the physical and spiritual center of most Bronze Age cultures is a pyramid of one kind or another, representing a symbolic mountain. In most cultures of this kind, the home of the Great Goddess was thought to be a mountain, the meeting place of heaven and earth. In the logic of the Bronze Age mind, there was an absolute identity between the Great Goddess and the mountain. As Adele Getty stated in *Goddess* (1990), "The Great Goddess is the Sacred Mountain." In the Stone Age, shrines were made inside her caves and on top of her peaks. With the origination of geometry as a sacred visual language during the Bronze Age, the geometric pyramid became the Sacred Mountain. In the highly metaphorical Bronze Age mindset, the pyramid *is* the Great Goddess.

The Goddess in Ancient Greece and Rome

The Iron Age was named for the capacity to make iron, which developed about three thousand years ago—

apparently first in what is now Turkey and later in East Asia. Within a short period, Indo-European barbarians on horseback invaded with iron weapons and transformed civilization, establishing the male-dominated society and theology that have characterized the West ever since. Despite such radical changes, there was considerable continuity between the divinities of the Bronze Age and the divinities of the Iron Age. Some of the most important cults moved from Minoan Crete to mainland Greece during the Bronze Age. One of the most important was the cult of Demeter and Persephone, which according to Greek mythology was taken to Eleusis by Theseus, first king of Athens, after he defeated the legendary Minotaur in the palace-temple of Crete at Knossos. By the fifth century B.C., this Eleusinian cult of the annual fruits of the earth had become so important that all the citizens of Athens participated in these rituals of eternal rebirth, and all Greeks were welcome to participate with them.

A theological harmony had been established during the Bronze Age between the Minoans and the Mycenaeans on the mainland. The highly civilized Minoans, who favored the Great Goddess, were largely responsible for civilizing the Mycenaeans, who had gone to the Greek mainland from the East, apparently from somewhere near Troy (in what is now Turkey). The Mycenaeans favored

Zeus, the sky god. Over time the pantheons merged, so that Zeus came to be regarded as the son of the Great Goddess of Crete, and Minoan goddesses such as Brito-martis probably became Athena or Artemis.

A psychosocial balance of male-female principles was firmly established in the Greek mind for centuries before the Dorian invasions ravaged the Greek mainland about three thousand years ago. The Dorians were hard-riding, hard-drinking barbarians whose iron weapons smashed the bronze weapons of the Mycenaeans. The Dorians had little use for goddesses; their divinities were ferocious males. It was they who crushed the goddess cults in particular, and civilization in general, throughout the whole of Greece. With the single exception of Athens, the Greek cities were burned to the ground. Civilization virtually ended. The centuries that followed are known as the Dark Ages of Greece (c. 1000-700 B.C.E.). Eventually, after generations of intermarriage, a form of theological compromise emerged. Zeus and other males would continue to dominate the pantheon, but goddesses would be permitted to play lesser roles. Thus, Hera and Aphrodite were allowed into heaven, but at a great price. Hera, once the Great Goddess of earth, became a bitchy wife. Aphrodite, once the Great Goddess of love and life, became a whore.

There were a few golden centuries for the goddesses of Greece, between the Dark Ages and the time people stopped believing in them or started reducing them to objects of gossip. During this period, from the sixth century B.C.E. to the second century B.C.E., the sculptors of Greece created some of the most beautiful images of goddesses that humankind has ever seen. It also was during this period that the Greeks produced some of the most impressive accomplishments in the entire history of architecture, ceramics, literature, philosophy, and government. Even though women were not allowed to be citizens, they nevertheless made very important contributions to this golden age. The poetry of Sappho holds its own beside that of her male peers. The teacher of Socrates is said to have been a woman named Diotima. Athenians were devoted, above all, to the goddess Athena, to whom they dedicated the Parthenon.

Over 90 percent of the Greek sculpture that survives is sacred. The Greeks of the golden age did not think of these as decorative objects. Like their Stone Age and Bronze Age ancestors, they believed that the spirits of the goddesses and the gods actually inhabited these sacred statues. There are reasons why figures such as the *Winged Victory of Samothrace* (page 223) are so famous today. They are much more than "pretty"; they are permeated by a dynamic spirituality, which can be rendered only by an artist who believes in the divinity being evoked.

The Romans copied much of the art and mythology of the Greeks while becoming civilized about two thousand years ago, just as the Mycenaeans had copied the Minoans one and a half millennia earlier. Brilliant administrators, engineers, soldiers, and writers, the Romans were much less gifted as sculptors. Greek goddesses lived on in the Roman Empire, but most Roman sculpture is merely a copy of a Greek prototype. Greek, Roman, and Egyptian goddess images were, in turn, the models that early Christians used for images of angels and for the Virgin Mary, who perpetuated many of the qualities of the Great Goddess.

The Goddess in the Hindu World

Most of us think of Greece and India as very far apart, and much has been written about their great differences, but it is also useful to consider what they have in common. Both had highly developed civilizations in the Bronze Age, and both probably had the Great Goddess as their spiritual center. Both goddess cultures were smashed, in the second millennium B.C.E., by Indo-Europeans who scorned all goddesses as minor. The native dark-skinned Dravidians, who had created Indian civilization, moved to the south of India to escape the Indo-Europeans; there they maintained their goddess-oriented culture. In the north, after generations of intermarriage, the Aryans (as the Indo-Europeans called themselves) eventually allowed goddesses to be part of their pantheon, but only in secondary positions.

At the end of the golden age of Greece, twenty-three centuries ago, Alexander the Great created an empire that reached to the Indus Valley, in northwestern India, where Indian civilization was flourishing again. Indian yogis started to visit Greece and were no doubt surprised to discover how much of their kind of philosophy seemed to have infused the Pythagorean-Platonic tradition of Greek thinking—perhaps through Babylonian descendants of the Sumerians, who had initiated Bronze Age civilization in Mesopotamia and perhaps also in the Indus Valley. There are arguments for the existence of a single "Indo-Sumerian" civilization about six thousand years ago. After the empire of Alexander the Great, Hellenistic Greek art had a profound influence on the art that arose from India's highly complex polytheism. Early statues of Buddha were carved under Greek influence, as were many Hindu statues.

The Dravidians of South India were not influenced in this way during the Greco-Indian era. They continued to build pyramid temples to their Great Goddess, who probably was envisioned in much the same way as she had been during the Stone Age. She has different names in different regions, but most often she is called Kali or Durga. She gives birth to life and dwells in the graveyards

Sri Yantra with Manifestations of the Great Goddess on All Sides. Nepal, c. 1700. Private collection.

to take it back again. Alone in the oldest myths, she later has a male partner; most often his name is Shiva.

Images of goddesses and gods are present in Bronze Age sites in India, as are images of a shamanlike figure seated in the classic position of yogic meditation. Then, as now, yogis and yoginis would meditate on the united nature of the goddess and god to attain cosmic consciousness. And then, as now, the most common work of art symbolizing this universal union was the Shiva linga—a phallic stone named from the male perspective, which fails to see its inherent female aspect. A more accurate description is the "linga-yoni." These simple, abstract shapes, based on male and female genitalia, usually appeared in conjunction during the classic era. The imagery is frankly sexual, but it uses sexual union as a metaphor for the cosmic oneness of the Great Goddess and the Great God. Thousands of these stone symbols appear throughout southern and northern India, both in simple roadside shrines and at the heart of the most elaborate temples.

In the north, primacy is given to the male, whether he is called Shiva, Vishnu, or Indra. But even in the north the Great God usually is shown in conjunction with his Shakti ("Energy"), his female aspect. It is Shiva and Shakti together who personify the primal principles of the universe: the motionless transcendent and the energy by which the transcendent moves through the material world. In many Hindu temples—especially in central India, where there was a merging of the Dravidian goddess and the Aryan god—the sacred architecture joins the phallic tower of the male principle with the triangular pyramid of the female principle in such a way that the two symbolic forms conjoin and rise toward heaven together.

Not all Hindu images symbolize the supreme conjunction; many celebrate the equally divine reality of the Great Goddess in her diverse aspects. From the early Vedic period, when the Aryan prayers were recorded in Sanskrit, are Usas (the dawn and the mother of cows), and Sarasvati, who began as a goddess of rivers and fertility and now is the graceful, purifying goddess of art, music, and learning. Also very popular is one of Shiva's best-known wives, Parvati, who was a mountain goddess. She now is seen as the ideal wife and mother, who brings the spirit of Shiva down to earth and into the household. Sometimes she appears alone or as the mother of Ganesha, and sometimes as the female half of the cosmic Androgyne, the divine male-female. This visual metaphor for nonduality has nothing to do with human bisexuality; the reference is to the ultimate goal of realizing a psychological integration of the goddess and the god within oneself.

The Goddess in Buddhism

The man we call Buddha was born in the sixth century
B.C.E. in that corner of India now known as Nepal. His
name was Siddhartha Gautama, but he came to be called
Shakyamuni ("Sage of the Shakyas," his people). He was
one of a number of remarkable men who transformed
religious and philosophical traditions during that pivotal
century, in which the individualistic cultural values of the
Iron Age crystallized. During those hundred years probably lived Lao-tzu in China, Buddha in India, Zoroaster in
Persia, Ezekiel in Mesopotamia, and Pythagoras in
Greece. Each turned the metaphysical tradition of his culture from semitribal to nontribal thinking. Until then, a
culture's tradition had been called simply "the way." Now,
many traditions are named for individuals. During the
Stone Age and the Bronze Age, the traditional way to be
at one with the infinite was by means of group rituals
intended to transcend ordinary reality. From the early
Iron Age to the present, the emphasis has been on individual experiences of the transcendent.

Buddha himself did not like the authoritarianism, elit-
ism, endless metaphysical speculation, and complex rituals
of Hinduism. He was interested in setting the mind free for
the direct experience of the here and now. Having managed to find his way into the eternal present, he wanted to
open others to this indescribable reality. It is probable that

the last thing he intended was to found another religion. He more likely wanted to start what Krishnamurti has described as a "philosophical tradition in which people teach themselves."

In fact, both a philosophical tradition (which is not a religion) and a religion grew out of his inspiration. Within the religion of Buddhism, many of the traditional symbols and divinities of Indian Hinduism spread throughout Asia, as Buddhism became an integral part of Tibet, Nepal, Southeast Asia, China, and eventually Japan. To a remarkable degree, the gods and goddesses of Buddhism became the "Light of Asia"—images through which the luminosity and wisdom of the infinite radiates. Buddhism usually did not replace the traditional animistic nature religions in these cultures but rather was grafted onto those spiritual roots as another way of knowing truth. Part of the reason Buddhism grew so quickly and spread so far is that its teachings were open to all, without discriminating against any gender, color, nationality, or socioeconomic class. That was revolutionary in a world that was highly conscious of all those factors.

The beautiful goddesses who dance in the minds of Buddhists do not need to be brought forth by group rituals or dances or drugs. In some Buddhist cults, all one needs to do is meditate correctly, and the goddess appears. No priests or priestesses are needed. Of the many goddesses in the

Buddhist pantheon, two of the most popular are Tara in Tibet and Kuan-Yin in China (known as Kannon in Japan); all three have many arms to serve the many needs of humanity. Tara means "Star." Said to have been born from the tears of her mate, Avalokiteshvara, she is the feminine embodiment of compassion. In her many manifestations, she can be peaceful or wrathful, depending on what best serves the need at hand. What Kuan-Yin and Kannon give to the people of China and Japan is constant, unconditional love, in ceaseless streams of radiance.

The goddesses of Buddhism have male partners. In tandem they represent the teaching that the female principle exists only in relationship with her counterpart and that the goal is that supreme state of being called androgyny. When contemplating an image of Buddha in a meditative vision or looking at a classic statue of Buddha, the two primary characteristics a follower perceives are the profoundly beautiful smile of gentle, all-loving wisdom and a body that looks male and female. The ultimate Buddhist goal of enlightenment is attained as each person comes to harmonize his or her own "feminine," intuitive compassion and "masculine," logical skills. The state of mind described as "nonduality" is referred to in the esoteric literature as the Sacred Marriage of all-loving wisdom and the knowledge of how to be of service to the world. Contemporary Buddhist teachers have said that nonduality can

SAICHI (active mid-13th century). *Sho Kannon with a
Body-of-Light Seated on a Lotus Holding the Lotus of Wisdom*,
1269. Bronze, partly gilded, height: 41⅛ in. (106.5 cm).
Museum of Fine Arts, Boston;
William Sturgis Bigelow Collection.

be understood as the harmonizing of the intuitive emotional capacities of the right brain with the analytical capacities of the left brain. In Tibetan Buddhism, this goal is symbolized in many ways, from the circle and square of the mandala to the Yab-Yum statues that show god and goddess in continuous sexual union. This metaphorical unity represents (as in Hinduism) the ultimate inseparability of the "male" and "female" forces of the universe.

The Goddess in Taoism

China is the oldest continuous civilization on earth. One of the most striking examples of continuity in the religious practice of China is the most holy temple of traditional China: the Temple and Altar of Heaven and Earth in Beijing, which until the start of this century was used to perform the shamanic ritual of the Sacred Marriage. This ritual is as old as China itself.

The native religion of China is Taoism, which—like Buddhism—is both a religion and a philosophical tradition apart from religion. Both aspects of Taoism have roots that go back to the Stone Age. In their modern form, the principles of Taoism are thought to have been crystallized by the great Chinese sage Lao-tzu. The little book of poetry *Tao-te Ching* (which may have been written by Lao-tzu alone or by a group of like-minded writers) is filled with such wisdom that it has been translated into more languages than any other book in history, except the Christian Bible. Lao-tzu's poetry, using male-female metaphors of the life forces united, has inspired the deepest of religious feelings—being at one with all that is.

The yin-yang principles that Lao-tzu drew on had been part of Chinese culture since the Neolithic era. Visual expressions of the yin and yang appear in many works of art of the Stone and Bronze Ages, symbolizing the divine male and the divine female in cosmic union. Typical is the sacred vessel called a *ts'ung,* which has a squared exterior and a circular interior; it is a three-dimensional mandala (as are many Asian temples). He is the circle, the infinite that activates. She is the square, the material world that is activated by the penetration of the eternal into the present. In Taoism (as in Buddhism and Hinduism), the circle and square in conjunction symbolize the nonduality of god and goddess, heaven and earth, spirit and matter.

Originally a Taoist Great Goddess, Kuan-Yin also became a Buddhist goddess after the interweaving of these two traditions in China during the first millennium C.E. Later, Zen developed from this merger in Japan. In both nations, Kuan-Yin blesses childbirth and endows wisdom. During the years of religious merging in China came some of the most beautiful images of the goddess ever painted. One of the best-known types was made by Mu-Ch'i (Fa-Ch'ang) during the Southern Sung dynasty and perpetuated by many Chinese and Japanese artists (page 239). Dressed in white and portrayed as the condensation of a gently luminous mist, Kuan-Yin is a profound visualization of matter as solidified spirit. A similar symbolism pervades the famous landscape paintings of the Sung period (in which misty clouds symbolize the goddess) and can even be seen in the bright white porcelain figures of Kuan-Yin that bless millions of Asian homes today.

As with all images of the Great Goddess, Kuan-Yin figures have many levels of meaning. In these pure white statues, as in the esoteric teachings of all the perennial traditions, the symbolism is of the unity of wisdom and love, as well as the parallel between the physical energy of white light and the metaphysical love that light carries into the physical world from the realm of the eternal.

THE GREAT GODDESS
Generator of All Creation

The oldest of all goddesses is known to historians of religion and mythology as the Great Goddess. She is the one supreme being, who was later subdivided into many lesser goddesses. She is all that existed at the beginning of time.

Art is widely believed to have been made first in Africa and then in Europe, when that region was first settled, perhaps forty thousand or fifty thousand years ago. When and where did the Great Goddess first appear in art? We will never know exactly, but it was sometime during the Old Stone Age. The earliest temples of the Great Goddess were caves; to be inside the great earth was to be within the Great Goddess.

In the oldest times, the Great Goddess had no name. One of the first names we know is Gaia, from the earliest creation myths of Greece. At least as old is Durga, in India (pages 60–61), and Nu-Wa, in China (page 85). In the best-known Paleolithic images, such as the *Goddess of Willendorf* (page 15), the Great Goddess is represented as a fertile, motherly female. People, animals, plants, sun, moon, and stars are all offspring of the Great Goddess. The *Goddess of Laussel* (opposite), who has features like those of the *Goddess of Willendorf,* holds a horn with thirteen marks, perhaps symbolizing phases of the moon. The *Goddess of Lespugue* (opposite) has the most exaggerated female features of all the known statues, reminding us that this art is primarily symbolic, not naturalistic. In other Stone Age images, the Great Goddess is represented as a slim young woman. This seems to be the "virginal" aspect, forever young, as continued in the myth of Demeter and Persephone—the same goddess in two aspects. Less well known are images of the Great Goddess as the Androgyne (pages 42, 44–46), in which the upper half of her body is a phallic symbol. She who is self-created and self-fertilizing is thus symbolized as being both female and male.

Goddess of Lespugue.
Old Stone Age, c. 30,000–20,000 B.C.E.
Mammoth ivory, height: 5½ in. (14 cm).
Musée de l'Homme, Paris.

Goddess of Dolni. Old Stone Age, c. 30,000–20,000 B.C.E.
Terra-cotta, torso height: 4¼ in. (11.5 cm).
Anthropological Institute, Brno, Czech Republic.

Goddess of Menton. Old Stone Age,
c. 30,000–20,000 B.C.E. Stone. Musée des Antiquités
Nationales, Saint-Germaine-en-Laye, France.

Goddess of Gagarino. Old Stone Age, c. 30,000-20,000 B.C.E.
Stone. Musée de l'Homme, Paris.

Goddess of Savignano. Old Stone Age, c. 30,000–20,000 B.C.E.
Serpentine, height: 8⅝ in. (21.8 cm).
Museo Preistorico ed Etnografico Luigi Pigorini, Rome.

Goddess Head. Cycladic, Late Stone or Early Bronze Age,
c. 2700–2400 B.C.E. Marble, height: 10⅝ in. (27 cm).
Musée du Louvre, Paris.

Goddess with a Child on Her Head. Cycladic, Late Stone or Early Bronze Age, 2700–2400 B.C F. Marble, height: 18⅛ in. (46 cm). Badisches Landesmuseum, Karlsruhe, Germany.

Goddess. Cycladic, Late Stone or Early Bronze Age, c. 2700–2400 B.C.E. Marble. Musée du Louvre, Paris.

Goddess, Probably Inanna, Holding Her Breasts. Sumerian,
c. 2000 B.C.E. Stone. Musée du Louvre, Paris.

Goddess or Priestess Holding Two Serpents. Minoan
(from Knossos), c. 1600–1500 B.C.E. Faience.
Archaeological Museum, Heraklion, Greece.

Goddess or Priestess Holding Two Serpents.
Minoan, c. 1600–1500 B.C.E.
Archaeological Museum, Heraklion, Greece.

*Goddess with Priestesses, Flowers, Bull Skulls, and
the Double-Axe Receiving the Young Sky God (Zeus?)*
(ring from Mycenae). Minoan, c. 1500 B.C.E.
Gold, National Archaeological Museum, Athens.

Goddess or Priestess Holding Two Serpents.
Minoan, c. 1600–1500 B.C.E.
Ivory and gold, height: 6⅜ in. (16.1 cm).
Museum of Fine Arts, Boston; Gift of Mrs. W. Scott Fitz.   53

Goddess.
Phoenicia, c. 700-600 B.C.E. Bronze and silver,
height: 7⅞ in. (20 cm). Musée du Louvre, Paris.

Mary Beth Edelson (b. 1933). *See for Yourself: Grapeva Neolithic Cave Ritual,* 1977. Time-release photograph of a performance at Grapeva Cave on Hvar Island, Yugoslavia.

55

THE GREAT GODDESS
Destroyer of All Creation

The Great Goddess is not only all-loving, all-giving, all-creating. She also is all-destroying. It is difficult for many to understand how the same goddess can be seen in such different ways, but the tribal mind is able to reconcile opposites more easily than the modern mind. What the modern analytical mind categorizes as a distinct duality, the tribal mind commonly perceives as an undivided unity of opposites. That way of thinking likens the Great Goddess to a boundless ocean of formless energy, which is always pregnant with the potential of becoming. Whatever exists pours out of this ocean of energy at the moment of creation and returns to this ocean of energy at the moment of death. Creation happens not once but continuously. So, too, does death. The cycle of nature never stops.

The paintings and sculpture of this goddess created during the historical period probably continue mythic images that go back to Stone Age origins. In India the earliest dated temples dedicated to Durga (pages 60-61) are carved of stone and built close to the earth, which is Durga's dwelling place. She *is* the earth. The symbolic shape of many of these temples is the pyramid. She *is* the pyramid. When the pyramidal, earth-hugging temple of the Great Goddess is designed in dynamic harmony with the great tower—symbol of the phallic verticality of the Great God, as in the world-famous medieval tantric temples in Orissa, India—the resulting unity of opposites produces a profound visual and spiritual experience.

In some cultures, sacred art stresses one aspect at a time, separating the Destroyer of All Creation from the Generator of All Creation in very dramatic ways. Among the most frightening images in all of art are those of Kali (pages 62–65). She is pictured in graveyards collecting bodies, on the bloody battlefield scavenging what remains of her children, and even killing her divine mate—the god Shiva. She destroys everything that is. If she did not, life itself could not continue. Only so much matter can exist in the world, and if that matter is not continuously recycled, life would ultimately stop.

Another terrifying image of the Great Goddess as destroyer was made by the Aztecs in Mexico about five hundred years ago. It is a giant stone statue of Coatlicue wearing a skirt of serpents and a necklace of skulls (page 68). Her head is composed as a double serpent, which is a common symbol for nonduality in the art of the Stone Age and the Bronze Age around the world. Coatlicue's architectural embodiment, like Durga's, was a pyramid. The power of this statue is so great that when it was dug up in Mexico City by archaeologists a century ago, they decided to put it back in the earth—an act almost unheard-of in archaeology. Having been unearthed again, it now is on view in the Instituto Nacional de Anthropologia e Historia in Mexico City. Coatlicue's child, Feathered Serpent (pages 70–71), symbolizes all that dies and is reborn. Farther north, in the land of the totem poles, in western Canada, the mythic role of destroyer/protector is played by Sisiutl (pages 74–75), the androgynous double serpent of the sea. Every culture has such mythic versions of how life becomes death and death, life.

Durga as Chamunda, Goddess of Destruction.
Nepal, 14th century. Bronze, height: 8 in. (20.3 cm).
Nappier Collection, Thiruvananthapuram, India.

Durga Killing the Buffalo Demon.
Eastern Ganga–Bhubaneswar, Orissa, India, second half
of 8th century. Sandstone with traces of red pigment,
27¼ x 16⅞ in. (69 x 43 cm). Philadelphia Museum of Art. 61

*Raja Surma Sen (r. 1781–88) and His Attendant Nagatu
in Worship of the Goddess.* Himachal Pradesh, India, 1785.
Opaque watercolor on paper, 7⅞ x 11⅝ in. (19.7 x 29.5 cm).
Los Angeles County Museum of Art;
Indian Art Special Purpose Fund.

A Procession with an Image of Kali.
West Bengal, India, 1850. Watercolor on mica,
6 x 7¾ in. (15.2 x 19.7 cm). Los Angeles County
Museum of Art; Gift of Miss Gertrude McCheyne.

Kali.
India, n.d. Indian Museum, Calcutta, India.

SUDHA MOOKERJEE (n.d.). *Goddess Kali,* 1954.
Tempera on paper, 36 x 24 in. (91 x 60.7 cm).
Priya Mookerjee.

Feathered Serpent (Kukulcan),
Son of Double Serpent, Receiving an Offering.
Limestone, 14⅞ x 32⅝ x 4⅛ in. (37.6 x 82.6 x 10.7 cm).
Mayan, 3d century. British Museum, London.

*Coatlicue (and/or Her Son) as the Double Serpent
Receiving an Offering* (detail from the *Codex Fejérvary-Mayer*).
Aztec, 15th–16th century. Gesso and paint on deerskin,
6⅜ x 6¾ in. (16.2 x 17.2 cm).
National Museums and Galleries on Merseyside, Liverpool
Museum, Liverpool, England; Donated by Joseph Mayer.   67

Coatlicue (from the Pyramid Court, Tenochtitlan).
Aztec, 14th–15th century. Stone.
Instituto Nacional de Antropologia e Historia, Mexico City.

Coatlicue. Aztec, 14th–15th century. Stone.
Instituto Nacional de Antropologia e Historia, Mexico City.

*Feathered Serpent (Quetzalcoatl), Son of Double Serpent
(Coatlicue), At One with Her Cosmic Power.* Aztec,
c. 14th–15th century. Stone. Musée de l'Homme, Paris.

Quetzalcoatl Rising from the Jaws of Death.
Aztec, c. 13th–15th century. Green jade.
British Museum, London.

Great Goddess (and/or Her Son) as the Double Serpent
(disk from Moundville). Mississippian culture,
c. 13th–16th century. Stone. Moundville Archaeological
Park, Moundville, Alabama.

Double-Serpent Dancers. Mississippian culture,
c. 13th–16th century. Shell. National Museum
of the American Indian, Smithsonian Institution.

Sisiutl, the Double Serpent, as a Soul-Catcher.
Tlingit, 19th century. Bone inlaid with abalone shell.
Provincial Museum, Victoria, Canada.

Sisiutl, the Double Serpent, on a Traditional Ceremonial Drum.
Kwakiutl, 19th–20th century. Skin on wood drum frame,
diameter: 15½ in. (39.2 cm); height: 3 in. (7.6 cm).
Vancouver Museum.

Gorgon. Greece, 6th century B.C.E. Stone.
Temple of Artemis, Corfu, Greece.

AUDREY FLACK (b. 1931). *Colossal Head of Medusa,* 1991.
Patinated and gilded bronze,
height (with base): 36 in. (91.4 cm). Collection of the artist.

PETER PAUL RUBENS (1577-1640). *Head of Medusa*, c. 1618.
Oil on canvas, 27 x 46¾ in. (68.5 x 118 cm).
Kunsthistorisches Museum, Vienna.

THE GREAT GODDESS-GOD
The Divine Androgyne

In many creation myths around the world, the creator is said to be a female so powerful that she does not need a male. In the ancient Greek pantheon, for example, Gaia conceived and gave birth without any male intervention. In other myths the creator is said to be a male so powerful that he does not need a female. Thus Zeus gave birth to Athena, who sprang, full-grown, from his forehead. As a rule, the gender of the solitary creator reflects the gender that is dominant in the culture. The first myths of Gaia were created at a time when women were highly respected, long before the Zeus-centered pantheon of classical Greece.

In many creation myths, the creator is said to be neither male nor female but both. Surveys of the Great Goddess that overlook this androgynous aspect neglect one of her most important features. Much of her greatness is due to being the supreme unity that transcends all opposites; she is the universal synthesis of all particulars. In popular mythology, she generates all; she is all matter that exists in space and time. Esoterically, she is both all that can be known and the knower; the knower and the known are one.

The sacred image of the Androgyne has been particularly difficult for modern people to comprehend. Those who encounter an image of the Androgyne today are somewhat like students of Zen contemplating a koan—reasoning does not work; comprehension requires intuition. The most famous androgynous images in Asian art are Hindu (page 88), and the image of the Great Goddess-God as one divine being remains very common throughout the tribal world today. Particularly well known is Nommo in Mali (pages 80, 90–91). The concept of the Androgyne continues in the esoteric teachings of the world religions—not only Taoism, Hinduism, and Buddhism but also esoteric Judaism, Christianity, and Islam. Historians of religion now think that all of these contemporary religions developed from the spiritual traditions of the tribal world of the Stone Age.

Androgyne is a term that comes from two Greek words; *andros* ("man") and *gyne* ("woman"). This term is the most accurate one available in English to describe the divided figure of the Great Goddess-God. Some writers describing this image use the term *hermaphrodite,* but that is a physical description of a human being who has the sexual organs of both a male and a female. The Great Goddess-God cannot be understood in such physical terms. The Androgyne is a metaphor that has nothing to do with any form of ordinary human sexual activity, be it heterosexual, homosexual, or bisexual.

The most common image of the Androgyne in the art of the Iron Age is not the vertical division (female below and male above) that is typical of the Stone Age (pages 44–45). It is a bilateral figure divided down the middle, male on the right side (the viewer's left) and female on the left (page 89). Interestingly, the female side of this universal image corresponds to the right brain, which controls the left side of the body, and the male side corresponds to the left brain, which controls the right side of the body. The central teaching of all such esoteric images is that the ultimate goal of the spiritual quest is androgyny, a state of mind in which the finite consciousness of the individual and the realm of the infinite cosmos are realized to be one. From the perspective of comparative world mythology, the consciousness of the Androgyne is identical with that of Buddha consciousness or Christ consciousness.

***Goddess and God (Ki and An?) in Cosmic Union as the
Double Serpent*** (libation cup of Gudea, Lord of Lagash).
Sumerian, c. 2000 B.C.E. Soapstone. Musée du Louvre, Paris.

Nu-Wa and Fu Xi in Cosmic Union as the Double Serpent.
China, 618-907. Color on cloth. British Museum, London.

*Paramasukha-Chakrasamvara and Chakrasamvara
in Cosmic Union.* Tibet, 17th century.
Gilt bronze, 12 x 10 x 4½ in. (30.5 x 25.4 x 11.4 cm).
Asian Art Museum of San Francisco;
Avery Brundage Collection.

Kalacakra and Vajradhara in Cosmic Union
(Lamaist temple banner). Tibet, 19th century.
Tempera on cotton, 24½ x 15 in. (62 x 38 cm).
By Courtesy of the Board of Trustees of
The Victoria and Albert Museum, London.

Ardhanarisvara (Hermaphroditic Shiva). Tiruvangado, India, 11th century. Madras Government Museum, Madras, India.

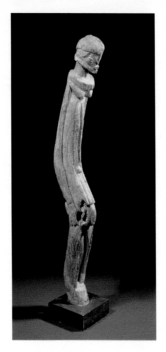

*Nommo, Cosmic Mother-Father of the Tribe
as the Androgyne, Standing.* Tellem tribe, Mali, n.d.
Wood. Musée de l'Homme, Paris.

Nommo, Cosmic Mother-Father of the Tribe. Dogon tribe,
Mali, 19th century. Wood, height: 22⅝ in. (57.8 cm).
University of Pennsylvania Museum, Philadelphia.

Mother and Father of the Tribe, Seated and Touching.
Dogon tribe, Mali, c. 19th century. Wood.
Barnes Foundation, Merion Station, Pennsylvania.

*Tutankhamen, the God-King, as the Androgyne
on a Leopard.* Egypt, 14th century B.C.E. Gilt wood.
Egyptian Museum, Cairo.

THE GREAT ANCESTOR
Mother of the Tribe

In the tribal worldview, every aspect of the natural world usually has its own spirit. Sometimes this invisible presence is so generalized that it is not named. However, when she has her own cult and is worshiped as a divine being powerful in her own right, she is described by historians of religion as a goddess, as opposed to a sprite or a nymph or a fairy. There are thousands of goddesses in the traditional world, so many that an encyclopedia would be required simply to list their names. This book can do no more than open the door into the realm of their mythic richness and mysterious beauty. Among the most important are those who can be grouped as the goddesses of motherhood, goddesses of the animals, goddesses of the fields, goddesses of love and sexuality, goddesses of health and healing, goddesses of war and victory, and goddesses of knowledge and wisdom. Each of these groups has its own chapter in this book.

This chapter is devoted to one who is probably older than all the others, having most likely emerged as a particularized aspect of the Great Goddess: the Great Ancestor, Mother of the Tribe. Many of the examples in this chapter are from Africa, which is probably where the first Great Ancestor images were created. Particularly powerful are statues such as the Ogboni goddess of the Yoruba in Nigeria, which reveal her connection with the animal world.

Ancestor worship, which is common in Asia as well as Africa, usually features communion with ancestors who go back for several generations, but not longer. They are often represented in sculptural figures that are also reliquaries holding the ashes of the departed. However, when we see a sculpture of a nude female in tribal art, such as the Afo goddess suckling (page 109), it usually represents not a typical ancestor figure but a very different, mythic being—either the Great Goddess or the Great Ancestor, Mother of the Tribe. Sometimes she is portrayed alone, sometimes with a child on her knee or at her breast. Sometimes (to make the symbolism more explicit), the suckling figure is an adult. There also are many figures of the first male ancestor and many works that depict the Mother of the Tribe and the Father of the Tribe together (page 92). As we have seen, celebrations of the unity of male and female principles are common in tribal art.

In many tribal societies, totemic animals (themselves usually part human and part animal) are honored as the first parents of the tribe. The most famous example of their Sacred Marriage in European mythology is the mating of the cow goddess and the bull god in Minoan Crete. Shamanic priests and priestesses dressed as various animal partners continued the Sacred Marriage ritual all over ancient Greece, and this ritual is still observed in many agricultural societies.

In many Stone and Bronze Age cultures, the queen is regarded as the personification of the Mother Goddess. Among the most beautiful statues of this type are the queen mothers of Nigeria and Egypt (page 99). No Egyptian "holy family" is more famous than Nefertiti and Akhenaton (page 98), the probable parents of King Tut. It was quite common for the Great Goddess of the Stone Age to change into a goddess of motherhood during the Iron Age. One of the best-known examples in the West is Hera, who became the loyal wife of Zeus and patron of mothers (page 111). One of the best-known Eastern examples is the dark-skinned Parvati, in India, who probably began life as the Great Goddess, then became domesticated as the partner of the Great God. There are also many images of Parvati in her own right, particularly in southern India (page 114), and as a member of the "holy family" (page 115).

*Akhenaton, Nefertiti, and Their Three Daughters
Praying to the Sun.* Amarna, Egypt, 14th century B.C.E. Stone,
17⅛ x 15⅜ in. (43.5 x 39 cm). Egyptian Museum, Cairo.

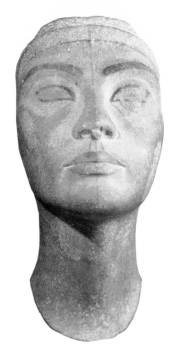

Nefertiti, the Goddess-Queen. Egypt, 14th century B.C.E. Stone. Egyptian Museum, Cairo.

Horus, Osiris, and Isis ("Triad of Osorkon").
Egypt, c. 889-866 B.C.E. Gold, lapis lazuli, and glass,
height: 3⅛ in. (9 cm). Musée du Louvre, Paris.

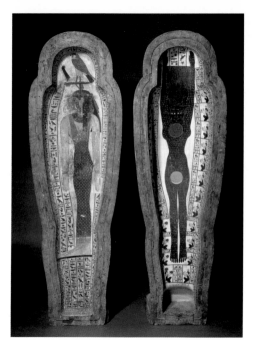

Nut [right], *Mother Goddess of the Sun God, Swallowing and Giving Birth to the Sun* (sarcophagus). Egypt, 7th century B.C.E. Rijksmuseum van Oudheden, Leiden, the Netherlands.

The "Capitoline Wolf" (with Romulus and Remus).
Etruscan, c. 500 B.C.E. Bronze, height: 33½ in. (85 cm).
Musei Capitolini, Rome.

BILL REID (b. 1920). *Bear Mother Suckling Her Two Cubs,*
1972. Gold. Canadian Museum of Civilization, Hull.

Goddess Tlazolteotl in Childbirth. Aztec, 14th–15th century.
Aplite with garnet inclusions, 8 x 4¾ x 5⅞ in.
(20.4 x 12.1 x 14.4 cm). Dumbarton Oaks, Research
Library and Collection, Washington, D.C.

First Ancestor. Admiralty Islands, c. 19th century. Wood.
Staatliches Museum für Volkerkunde, Munich.

First Ancestor with Horns.
Ogboni Society, Yoruba tribe, Nigeria, c. 19th century.
Wood. National Museum, Lagos, Nigeria.

Royal Ancestor, the Divine Queen Mother.
Bini tribe, Benin City, Nigeria, early 16th century. Bronze,
Height: 20 in. (50.8 cm). National Museum, Lagos, Nigeria. 107

First Ancestor Holding Her Breasts. BaLuba tribe, Zaire,
c. 19th century. Wood and hide, height: 17½ in. (44.3 cm).
British Museum, London.

First Ancestor Suckling a Child. Afo tribe, Africa,
c. 19th century. Wood, 27⅝ x 11⅞ x 12¼ in.
(70 x 30 x 31 cm). The Horniman Museum, London.

The Goddess Hera Between Two Lions.
Greece, early 7th century B.C.E. Stone.
National Archaeological Museum, Athens.

Hera and Zeus (metope from the "E" temple at Selinus).
Greece, 5th century B.C.E. Marble.
Museo Archeologico, Palermo, Italy.

Tellus, Goddess of Earth. Roman, 1st century B.C.E.
Marble. Museo Ara Pacis Augustae, Rome.

Daedalus and Pasiphaë. Roman, 1st century.
Wall painting. House of the Vettii, Pompeii, Italy.

Parvati. Tamil Nadu, India, early 11th century. Copper alloy,
height: 35 in. (88.9 cm). Asia Society, New York;
Mr. and Mrs. John D. Rockefeller 3rd Collection.

Shiva and Parvati. Tamil, India, 12th century. Copper alloy,
19 x 23¾ in. (48.3 x 60.3 cm). Asia Society, New York;
Mr. and Mrs. John D. Rockefeller 3rd Collection.

GEORGES LACOMBE (1868–1916). *Isis*, c. 1895.
Partially polychromed mahogany, 43⅝ x 24⅜ x 3⅞ in.
(111 x 62 x 10 cm). Musée d'Orsay, Paris.

Frida Kahlo (1907-1954). *My Nurse and I,* 1937.
Oil on sheet metal, 11¾ x 13¾ in. (29.8 x 34.9 cm).
Fundacion Dolores Olmedo, Mexico City.

GODDESSES OF THE ANIMALS

The vast majority of images painted in the sacred caves of the Old Stone Age are animals. Usually they are images of the animals that a tribe hunted or the animals they regarded as their totems. (Sometimes it is a taboo to eat totem animals, sometimes not.) We can never know exactly the meaning of the symbolism in cave paintings that are twenty or thirty thousand years old. However, we know enough about how the Stone Age people of today think and act to have a general sense of why these paintings were made.

It is widely believed that these are shamanic scenes that embody the spirits of the animals to be hunted. Symbolically killing these images first would ensure the success of the hunt, if the correct magic rituals were conducted as well—rituals in which the animals would be asked to give their life so that the tribe might live and rituals that thanked the animals for their sacrifice. These Stone Age "temples" were likely also used for initiation ceremonies.

Also found in such sacred caves are sculpted and painted images of the Great Goddess, from whose being the animals take life. In Neolithic cultures the Mistress of the Animals (a younger female deity), rather than the Great Goddess, commonly presided over the animals.

Perhaps the most depicted example of such a goddess is the Greeks' Artemis (Diana in the Roman pantheon; pages 118, 132–35). There are as many different versions of the Mistress of the Animals as there were sacred creatures to whom she was protector. She is thought of sometimes as guardian of all animals, sometimes of only one animal. Frequently, she started as the totemic mother animal of a band or tribe. In Bronze Age cultures she often became a human-animal aspect of the Great Goddess. It is typical of Bronze Age deities to be part animal and part human—a shamanic synthesis of two aspects within one being. Among the best-known goddesses of this type, in North America and in Egypt, are such totemic mergers as Spider-Woman, Neith-Cobra (page 123), Hathor-Cow (page 125), and Selket-Scorpion (page 131). Later, in the Iron Age, came a visual separation of goddess and animal, as with Cybele and the lions, Athena and the owl, and Aphrodite and the swan. It is typical of Iron Age deities to be entirely human, with their creatures beside them as shamanic spirit allies who give their power to the deity.

Mut and Neith (from the tomb of Tutankhamen).
Egypt, 14th century B.C.E. Egyptian Museum, Cairo.

Buto (Uazit), Cobra Goddess. Egypt, 664–610 B.C.E.
Limestone, 16⅞ x 4½ x 11 in. (43 x 11 x 28 cm).
University of Pennsylvania Museum, Philadelphia.

Neith, Cobra Goddess (from the tomb of Tutankhamen).
Egypt, c. 1325 B.C.E. Gilt wood. Egyptian Museum, Cairo.

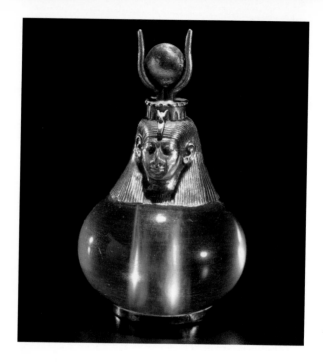

Spherical Amulet with Head of the Goddess Hathor.
Nubia, c. 747-716 B.C.E. Rock crystal and gold, height: 2½ in.
(5.3 cm). Museum of Fine Arts, Boston; Museum Expedition.

Hathor, Cow Goddess. Saqqara, Egypt, 7th–6th century B.C.E.
Stone. Egyptian Museum, Cairo.

Bast, Cat Goddess. Saqqara, Egypt, after 600 B.C.E.
Bronze, with inlaid silver and gold, 15 x 5⅛ in. (38 x 13 cm).
British Museum, London.

Bast, Cat Goddess. Egypt, n.d. Bronze, height: 24 in. (61 cm).
The Field Museum, Chicago.

Tauret, Hippopotamus Goddess. Egypt, n.d.
Basalt, height: 16⅜ in. (41.5 cm).
The Field Museum, Chicago.

Sekhmet, Lion Goddess (from the Temple of Mut, Karnak).
Egypt, c. 930 B.C.E. Black granite. Musée du Louvre, Paris.

Selket, Scorpion Goddess. Egypt, c. 1570–332 B.C.E.(?).
Bronze. Musée du Louvre, Paris.

Selket, Scorpion Goddess (from the tomb of Tutankhamen).
Egypt, 14th century B.C.E. Gilt wood.
Egyptian Museum, Cairo.

Artemis.
Etruscan, 6th century B.C.E. Ceramic, height: 26 in. (66 cm).
Museo Archeologico, Florence.

THE PAN PAINTER (n.d.). *Artemis and Actaeon:*
Attic Red-Figure Krater. Greece, c. 470 B.C.E.
Ceramic, 14⅝ x 16⅝ in. (37 x 42 cm). Museum of Fine Arts,
Boston; James Fund and by Special Contribution.

Diana of Ephesus. Roman, c. 1st–3d century.
Bronze, blackened bronze, and alabaster.
Museo Archeologico Nazionale, Naples.

Rape of Europa. Greater Greece, c. 600 B.C.E. Stone.
Museo Archeologico, Palermo, Italy.

TITIAN (c. 1488–1576). *Europa*, 1562.
Oil on canvas, 70⅝ x 81¼ in. (178.7 x 205.5 cm).
Isabella Stewart Gardner Museum, Boston.

HENRI ROUSSEAU (1844–1910). *The Dream*, 1910.
Oil on canvas, 80½ x 117½ in. (204.5 x 298.5 cm).
The Museum of Modern Art, New York;
Gift of Nelson A. Rockefeller.

LAUREL BURCH (b. 1945). *Spirit of the Goddess: One World, Many Voices*, 1995. Watercolor on paper, 40 x 60 in. (101.6 x 152.4 cm). Private collection.

REMEDIOS VARO (1908–1963).
Creation of the Birds, 1958. Oil on Masonite, 20⅝ x 24⅝ in.
(52.3 x 62.5 cm). Private collection.

LOUISE BOURGEOIS (b. 1911). *The She-Fox,* 1985.
Marble, 56½ x 20 x 30 in. (143.5 x 50.8 x 76.2 cm).
Private collection, Boston.

GODDESSES OF THE FIELDS,
FLOWERS, AND TREES

If one of the first particularizations of the Great Goddess was the goddess of the animals, one of the next must have been the goddess of the fields. As soon as agriculture was developed (probably by women), about ten thousand years ago, Neolithic culture emerged. Wandering tribes of hunter-gatherers settled into villages, where they farmed and raised animals, often to supplement their traditional hunting. In these societies, and in their counterparts still surviving today, no deity is more important than the goddess of the fields.

Best known among them are the goddesses of corn, which has been the primary food supply in much of the world for many centuries. In some societies, the deity of corn is known simply as Corn Mother. Where other crops are raised, as in North America, the deities of beans and squash are frequently called Sisters of Corn Mother. In more complex literate societies, such goddesses have personal names. As a goddess of the harvest in the ancient Near East she was called Astarte (pages 150-52) and Ishtar; she is known as Ala in Nigeria (page 172), Annapurna in India, Chicomecoatl or Tonantzin in Aztec Mesoamerica (page 170), Hainuwele in New Guinea,

Taranga in Polynesia, and Selu among the Cherokee—to cite just a few. The goddess of the fields is very much alive among the millions of people who still live according to traditional ways.

In Greece the goddess of the fields was given two names, for her two aspects: Demeter (pages 154–58) is the mother who never dies; Persephone (page 159–63) is the daughter who descends into death's underworld but returns to life each year. (On page 160 Persephone is seen with her underworld husband, Hades.) The most famous celebration of the Greek corn rituals was at Eleusis, near Athens. Although few details are known about the Eleusinian ritual, we do know that what was reborn each year, probably following a Sacred Marriage, was corn.

The Great Goddess was also frequently particularized as a goddess of individual flowers and trees. Many have had and still have their own cult. In Japan, Aze is the spirit of the pine tree. In China, Hsi Wang Mu is the spirit of the peach tree. In the Near East, the myrrh tree is Myrrha. In the Balkans, Kupalo is the birch tree. In Ireland, Buan's loving tears became the hazel tree. In Greece, Daphne, a virgin priestess of Gaia, was turned into a laurel tree to protect her from the ardent embraces of Apollo (pages 168–69). Among the Iroquois of North America, Oniata was said to have been so beautiful that she was a danger to her tribes' marriages, so she transformed herself into the wildflowers of the spring. Among the Aztecs, Xochiquet-zal was the goddess of flowers, particularly the marigold. She has much in common with the Roman flora (page 142), who is the best known of all floral goddesses. Each spring both goddesses were at the center of orgiastic festivals of world renewal. One European version was the festival of the maypole. The pole was the traditional symbol of the male deity who would impregnate Mother Earth every year in the ritual of the Sacred Marriage.

Goddess Ritual of Death and Regeneration
(sarcophagus from Hagia Triada). Minoan, c. 1400 B.C.E.
Archaeological Museum, Heraklion, Greece.

The Flotilla Fresco, Goddess Festival of the Sea
(detail, left side). Minoan, c. 1500 B.C.E. Wall painting.
National Archaeological Museum, Athens.

The Flotilla Fresco, Goddess Festival of the Sea
(detail, right side). Minoan, c. 1500 B.C.E. Wall painting.
National Archaeological Museum, Athens.

Goddess of Growth (Astarte?) with Two Serpents (pendant). Ugarit, Phoenicia, 15th century B.C.E. Gold. Musée du Louvre, Paris.

Goddess of Growth (Astarte?) Wearing a Serpentine Coil.
Ugarit, Phoenicia, c. 18th century B.C.E. Ivory.
Musée du Louvre, Paris.

Astarte. Seleucid Empire, c. 2d century B.C.E.
Alabaster. Musée du Louvre, Paris.

DANTE GABRIEL ROSSETTI (1828–1883). *Astarte Syriaca,* 1877.
Oil on canvas, 72 x 42 in. (182.2 x 106.2 cm).
City Art Gallery, Manchester, England.

Goddess (Demeter?) with Grain and Goats
(cosmetic-box cover). Ugarit, Phoenicia, 13th century B.C.E.
Ivory, height: 5⅜ in. (13.7 cm). Musée du Louvre, Paris.

Goddess (Demeter?) Enthroned, Receiving Offerings
(ring from Tiryns). Mycenaean, c. 16th century B.C.E. Gold.
National Archaeological Museum, Athens.

Demeter and Persephone (?).
Minoan-Mycenaean, 14th–13th century B.C.E. Ivory.
National Archaeological Museum, Athens.

*Demeter Holding Grain and Poppy Pods
Between Serpents.* Greece, c. 3d–2d century B.C.E.
Terra-cotta. Museo Nazionale delle Terme, Rome.

157

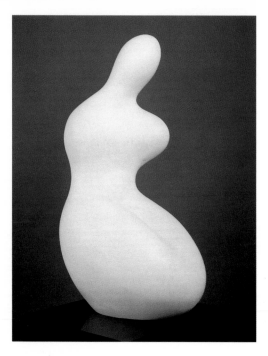

JEAN ARP (1886–1966). *Demeter*, 1960.
Marble. Private collection.

Persephone (from the Dipylon, Athens). Greece, c. 730 B.C.E.
Ivory. National Archaeological Museum, Athens.

Persephone and Hades in the Underworld.
Etruscan, c. 480–450 B.C.E. Terra-cotta.
Museo Nazionale, Reggio Calabria, Italy.

Persephone in a Dorian Peplos.
Greece, 6th century B.C.E.
Acropolis Museum, Athens.

MARY FRANK (b. 1933). *Persephone*, 1985.
Terra-cotta, 25 x 74 x 38 in. (63.2 x 187.2 x 96.1 cm).
The Metropolitan Museum of Art, New York;
Courtesy of D. C. Moore Gallery and the artist.

LAUGHING WATER (b. 1940). *Persephone Rising,* 1994.
Painted print, 11 x 8½ in. (27.9 x 21.6 cm).
Art Information Center, Northbank, California.

Goddess of Growth.
Bulandibagh, India, 3d–2d century B.C.E.
Patna Museum, Bihar, India.

Ambika, Goddess of Growth, Wife of Shiva.
Orissa, India, c. 1000. Stone, 20⅜ x 10½ x 5½ in.
(51.5 x 26.5 x 14 cm). By Courtesy of the Board of Trustees
of The Victoria and Albert Museum, London.　165

Goddess of Growth. Mathura School, India,
c. 2d century. Terra-cotta.
Musée des Arts Asiatiques Guimet, Paris.

MIN CHEN (n.d.). *Ma-Ku*, early 19th century.
Paper mounted on silk, 36⅛ x 67½ in. (92 x 171.5 cm).
The Field Museum, Chicago.

ANTONIO DEL POLLAIUOLO (c. 1432–1498). *Apollo and Daphne,*
c. 1470–80. Oil on wood, 11⅝ x 7⅞ in. (29.5 x 20 cm).
The National Gallery, London.

GIANLORENZO BERNINI (1598–1680). *Apollo and Daphne*,
1622–24. Marble, height: 96 in. (243 cm).
Museo Borghese, Rome.

Tonantzin. Aztec, 14th–15th century.
Ceramic, 4¾ x 2 x 1⅞ in. (12 x 5 x 4 cm).
British Museum, London.

Xochiquetzal, Goddess of Love, Flowers, and Dancing
(detail from *Codex Borbonicus*). Aztec, c. 1500.
Bibliothèque de l'Assemblée Nationale, Paris.

Ala, Goddess of Growth. Ogowe, Gabon, n.d.
Wood, height: 43¾ in. (111 cm).
The Field Museum, Chicago.

AUGUSTE RODIN (1840–1917). *Eternal Springtime*,
c. 1884. Bronze. Philadelphia Museum of Art;
Given by Paul Rosenberg.

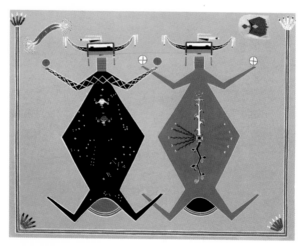

FRANC J. NEWCOMB (1889–1970). *Male Shootingway,
the Blue Mother Earth, and Black Father Sky*, c. 1930.
Traditional sand painting, Kayenta, Arizona, 22 x 28½ in.
(55.6 x 72.1 cm). Courtesy of The Wheelwright Museum
of the American Indian, Santa Fe, New Mexico.

WALDO MOOTZKA (1910–1940). *Pollination of the Corn,* n.d.
Tempera on paper, 12 x 8½ in. (30.5 x 21.6 cm).
Gilcrease Museum, Tulsa, Oklahoma.

GODDESSES OF LOVE AND SEXUALITY

No goddess has had a greater appeal to the modern imagination than the goddess of love—known by her Greek name, Aphrodite, and more popularly by her Roman name, Venus. Although her many cults probably started as typical fertility cults—devoted to the rebirth of plants, animals, and people—she was redefined by the Greeks into an image of ideal beauty and powerful love. In the decadent years toward the end of Greece's dominance, she also became a symbol for all that makes men lust. The ancient story of how Venus was conceived in a mystical union of the sky god and the watery earth goddess has been forgotten by most people, but her naked body remains an embodiment of the boundless love for which humans never stop yearning. From ancient Greece to Renaissance Europe, Venus symbolized two kinds of love—the lusting love of ordinary consciousness and the chaste, selfless love of higher consciousness.

The most familiar Venus images are the Greek statues, particularly the *Venus de Milo* (page 187). Such sculpture also fired the imagination of artists in Renaissance Europe and helped shape the modern image of the ideal nude. The Neo-Platonic artists of the Renaissance continued the Greek distinction between two kinds of love, perceiving the love for physical beauty as a stepping stone in elevating one's awareness toward the realization of divine beauty.

Painters and sculptors have been haunted by the image of Venus as the most beautiful of all women, and no goddess has been reiterated in Western art more often than she. Sandro Botticelli, at the Neo-Platonic court of Florence, managed to render a nude that is both physical and metaphysical (page 190). Giorgione and Titian (pages 188–89) moved perception toward the physical. Aristide Maillol returned to the ancient ideal of the physical as symbolic of the metaphysical (page 255). Andy Warhol created an image well suited to an age that has nearly lost its sense of the sacred (page 191).

Venus has parallels in traditional cultures on every inhabited continent. In northern Europe she was Var, or Frigga (also known as Freya) (page 194), or Frigga's daughter Hnossa. In Wales, she was Branwen, the "White-Breasted One," whose totem was the white crow. In the ancient Near East, her name was Ishtar ("Light-Giving"), the moon goddess, or Astarte, the evening star (pages 150–52). The Scythians called her Artimpassa, goddess of the moon. In India she was evoked by calling out the name of Radha, who is sensuality personified (page 183)—not simply a physical sensuality but a tantric sensuality intended to link her worshipers with divinity.

This concept of sexuality as a path to the transcendent was far-reaching. In Mesopotamia the temples of the goddess were the homes of priestesses who offered sex in the hope that it would help the faithful enter the realm of the holy.

As the modern world has lost touch with the original meaning of Venus and has lost most of its sense of true mythology, Venus images have become empty shells. Thanks to Hollywood films, men's magazines, and porno flicks, the word *goddess* has become trivialized to mean little more than naked ladies representing the fantasies of males whose experience of ecstasy is limited to a brief sexual spasm. Gone is the magic that filled the hearts of our ancient ancestors, who saw in Venus a gateway to permanent ecstatic oneness with the eternal.

Kandariya-Mahadeva Temple (north facade).
Khajoraho, India, 10th–11th century. Sandstone.

Torso of Fertility Goddess (Yakhsi) (from a gateway of stupa, no. 1, Sanchi). Madhya Pradesh, India, c. 25. Sandstone, height: 28⅜ in. (72 cm). Museum of Fine Arts, Boston; Gift of Denman Waldo Ross Collection.

Apsara Combing Her Hair. Khmer, Cambodia, n.d.
Musée des Arts Asiatiques Guimet, Paris.

Radha and Krishna in the Grove. Kangra School, Punjab,
India, c. 1780. Gouache on paper, 4⅞ x 6¾ in.
(12.3 x 17.2 cm). The Victoria and Albert Museum, London.

Aphrodite Rising from the Sea.
Greece, 6th–5th century B.C.E. Marble.
Museo Nazionale delle Terme, Rome.

Aphrodite ("Venus Genetrix"). 5th–4th century B.C.E.
Antique copy of a Greek work attributed to Callimachus.
Marble, height: 67¾ in. (171.3 cm). Musée du Louvre, Paris.

Aphrodite of Cnidus. C. 350 B.C.E. Roman copy
of a Greek work attributed to Praxiteles.
Marble, height: 48 in. (122 cm). Musée du Louvre, Paris.

Aphrodite ("Venus de Milo").
Melos, Greece, c. 100 B.C.E. Marble, height: 79½ in. (202 cm).
Musée du Louvre, Paris.

GIORGIONE (1477–1510). *Sleeping Venus.* c. 1508–10.
Oil on canvas, 42⅞ x 69⅛ in. (108.5 x 175 cm).
Gemäldegalerie, Staatliche Kunstsammlungen, Dresden, Germany.

TITIAN (1488/89–1576). *The Venus of Urbino*, c. 1538.
Oil on canvas, 46½ x 65 in. (119 x 165 cm).
Galleria degli Uffizi, Florence.

SANDRO BOTTICELLI (1445–1510). *Birth of Venus*, c. 1484–86.
Tempera on canvas, 68¼ x 110 in. (172.5 x 278.5 cm).
Galleria degli Uffizi, Florence.

ANDY WARHOL (1930-1987). *Detail of Renaissance Paintings
(Sandro Botticelli, "Birth of Venus," 1482)*, 1984.
Screenprints, 32 x 44 in. (80.9 x 111.3 cm), each.
Courtesy Edition Schellmann, Munich/NY. 191

Jean-Auguste-Dominique Ingres (1780-1867).
Venus Anadyomène, 1867. Oil on canvas, 11½ x 7½ in.
(29 x 19 cm). Musée Condé, Chantilly, France.

ODILON REDON (1840–1916). *The Birth of Venus*, 1912.
Oil on canvas, 32⅞ x 25¼ in. (83 x 64 cm).
Musée du Petit Palais, Paris.

Frigga (?) (bowl from Gundestrup, Denmark).
Celtic Iron Age, c. 500–1 B.C.E.
Silver, height: 8 in. (20 cm); diameter: 9⅜ in. (24 cm).
National Museum, Copenhagen.

PAUL KLEE (1879-1940). *Barbarians' Venus*, 1921.
Oil, oil transfer, and opaque watercolor on plaster-coated
gauze on painted board, 16⅛ x 10½ in. (40.9 x 26.7 cm).
The Norton Simon Museum, Pasadena, California;
Blue Four Galka Scheyer Collection, 1953.

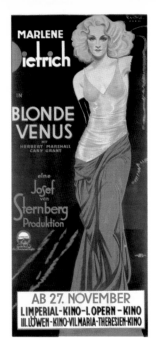

VOGL. *Poster for the Film "Blonde Venus,"* 1932.
Private collection.

NIKI DE SAINT PHALLE (b. 1930). *Black Venus,* 1965–67.
Painted polyester, 110 x 35 x 24 in. (279.4 x 88.9 x 61 cm).
Whitney Museum of American Art, New York;
Gift of the Howard and Jean Lipman Foundation, Inc.   197

GODDESSES OF HEALTH AND HEALING

The first healers were the shaman and the shamaness. Virtually every tribal group known today has a shaman or a shamaness, so it is probable this has been the case since time immemorial. Sometimes male shamans are more common within a tribe; sometimes female shamans are more common. They do not deal with minor problems, since there are numerous minor deities who can be called on to assist with headaches, bellyaches, and so on. Shamanic skills are reserved for major ills, such as a serious psychological disorder, an attack by a witch, soul theft by a sorcerer, or metaphysical danger to the entire community.

In less complex cultures, the shaman usually works alone, often in a trance state. In more complex cultures, societies of healers often work collectively. Shamanesses have been dominant in many regions, such as the Hupa tribe in northern California and all over Korea today. In West Africa, among the Mende, shamanic priestesses are organized into powerful societies called Sande and Yassi. They are the only females in Africa who wear ritual masks made just for them (pages 206–9), and the only females in the tribal world who are known to take turns with men in the administration of tribal affairs. They also commission powerful figure sculpture (opposite and page 205). All shamanic healers selflessly draw on the power of a goddess or god, becoming conduits for the power of higher energies.

The more complex a society becomes, the more specialized its goddesses of health and healing become. At first there usually are generalized goddesses of well-being, such as the Greeks' Iris (page 213), who transported the healing power of the Mother Goddess to earth on the rainbow. She carried with her the caduceus—the staff with two entwined serpents that has symbolized wholeness since the Stone Age. Modern medicine still uses this image as a symbol of health and wellness. Hermes took this symbol from Iris and taught healing to Asklepios, who in turn taught his daughter, the goddess Hygeia ("Health") (pages 210-12). Harmonia ("Harmony"), the healer, was the daughter of Aphrodite and Ares (love and war).

Every society has its own vision of how the goddess heals. In India, Ganga is so old that she has no human form. Half of her lives in the river of light that is the Milky Way; half of her lives in the river of water that is the Ganges, in whose holy currents millions wash away the illnesses of this life and past lives. Working with Ganga is Sitala, who cures smallpox, and Sushumma, the "fire in the spine" that rises up to the skull to heal an unbalanced mind. In Nigeria, among the Yoruba, Oshun is the healing river; her following has spread to Central and South America. In Korea, Pali Kongju is the ancestor of all women shamans, who are known as Mudang.

She knows how to fly through the heavens and how to bring the dead to life, as do all shamanic deities.

Among the early Jews, Sarah, the greatest of Hebrew matriarchs (and possibly a Chaldean priestess), was the wife and sister of Abraham. In the Old Testament (Genesis 17:16), God describes her as "mother of nations." Her very presence gave health to the Jews and fertility to both the Jews and the Egyptians. As delineated in Savina Teubal's *Sarah the Priestess* (1984), Sarah has many of the traits of a Near Eastern goddess of fertility and healing—the type represented on the "Astarte plaques" now being dug from the soil of Israel (page 150). These fertility amulets were worn as pendants. The spirit personified by the wife of Abraham has continued in Judaism as Shekhinah, the "radiance of God" who arrives "like a bride" every week on the Sabbath, to regularly restore the feeling of spiritual wholeness. Esoterically, Shekhinah is regarded as the feminine aspect of God, who dwells inside every individual.

Among Christians, Brigid (Briganta, Bride)— "Bright One"—is venerated as an Irish saint, but originally she was an extremely powerful Celtic goddess of healing, worshiped in Ireland, Scotland, England, and France. Her transformation from goddess to saint offers one of the clearest examples of how Christianity systematically assimilated and transformed into a saint virtually every major goddess of the pre-Christian world.

Goddess (headdress mask).
Bini tribe, Benin City, Nigeria, c. 1800.
Brass, height: 14½ in. (36.7 cm). British Museum, London.

Male Partner of the Goddess (headdress mask).
Bini tribe, Benin City, Nigeria, c. 1800.
Brass, height: 27¼ in. (69 cm). British Museum, London.

203

Nowa. Yassi Society, Mende tribe, Sierra Leone,
c. 19th century. Wood, 47¼ x 7 x 7½ in. (120 x 18 x 19 cm).
British Museum, London.

Goddess with Ram Horns (libation cup to be used only by
the king). Bakuba tribe, Zaire, c. 19th century. Wood,
height: 10¾ in. (27 cm). British Museum, London.

Nowa (helmet mask). Yassi Society or Sande Society, Mende tribe, Sierra Leone, c. 19th century. Wood, height: 14 in. (35.4 cm). Buffalo Museum of Science.

Nowa (helmet mask). Gola tribe, Sierra Leone,
c. 19th century. Wood and metal, 14 x 7½ x 9 in.
(35.6 x 19 x 22.9 cm). Harn Museum,
University of Florida, Gainesville; Gift of Rod McGalliard.

Nowa (helmet mask). Mende, Gola, or Vai tribe, Sierra Leone, c. 19th century. Wood, 15⅜ x 7⅞ x 8¾ in. (38.9 x 20 x 22 cm). Harn Museum, University of Florida, Gainesville; Gift of Rod McGalliard.

Nowa (helmet mask). Gola or Vai tribe, Sierra Leone,
c. 19th century. Wood and metal, 32½ x 14¾ x 13⅝ in.
(82.5 x 37.5 x 34.5 cm). Harn Museum,
University of Florida, Gainesville; Gift of Rod McGalliard.

Hygeia and Asklepios. Roman copy of a Greek work from
4th century B.C.E. Marble. Vatican Museum, Rome.

Asklepios and Hygeia. Roman, c. 400–430. Ivory, 12⅜ x 5½
in. (31.4 x 13.9 cm). National Museums and Galleries on
Merseyside, Liverpool Museum, Liverpool, England;
Donated by Joseph Mayer.   211

AUDREY FLACK (b. 1931). *Islandia, Goddess of the Healing Waters*, 1987. Polychromed and gilded plaster, 66½ x 38 in. (168.9 x 96.5 cm). Collection of the artist.

AUGUSTE RODIN (1840–1917). *Iris.* Bronze.
Musée Rodin, Paris.

GODDESSES OF WAR AND VICTORY

War has been a regular part of life among people of the Iron Age, in which most of us are still living. Peaceable exceptions are rare. But the historical record is filled with examples of peaceful, goddess-oriented societies that were invaded and conquered by god-oriented warriors. In the process, the old Mother Goddess often was turned into a warrior goddess. Nevertheless, in some cases there tended to be a continuing reverence for the Mother Goddess, above all others, in her original aspect as the sacred center of all being. Consider the case of Gaia, who was Mother Earth in Greece before the warriors came. The story was told of how she was the Primary One, who came from the formless void and then gave birth to Chronos (time) and Uranus (space). Even the warriors of classical Greece swore their oaths on the sacred name of Gaia, though their primary allegiance was elsewhere.

Many warrior societies had a war goddess whose name was invoked before each battle. Aeron was Welsh. Agasaya was Semitic. Andraste was Celtic. Ankt was Egyptian. Badb was Irish. Bellona was Roman. Hariela was German. Sroya was Slavic. Sinjang Halmoni was Korean. And the wild Valkyries fought with the Scandi-navians on flying horses and carried away the slain. They are among the few Scandinavian goddesses who are still widely remembered.

Today the most familiar war goddess is Athena, protector of Athens. The goddess in all her many forms was particularly powerful in Athens, where the Great Goddess of the Minoan-Mycenaean world had once lived. Athens was the only Greek city-state that was not conquered by the last great wave of Indo-European invaders. And only in Athens was the spirit of the goddess neither crushed nor trivialized. The most famous of all Greek temples, the Parthenon, was built for Athena. Inside it stood her image in the form of one of the largest of all Greek statues (forty feet tall and clothed with gold), where her spirit was said to dwell (page 221).

Like many important goddesses, Athena is a complex deity with many aspects. Originally, she probably was most closely associated with the wisdom tradition of a peaceful agricultural cult, quite possibly Minoan. She never stopped being a goddess of wisdom, even after she also became a goddess of war. In this chapter are images of her as the warrior who guided the Athenians to many victories (page 214). In the next chapter are images of her as the Wise One (page 232).

Nothing was more important to the warrior societies of Greece and Rome than victory in war. Victoria (which means Victory; her Greek name is Nike) and many other deities eventually emerged as separate goddesses of victory. The best-known statue of Nike is the *Winged Victory of Samothrace* (page 223), now in the Louvre in Paris. It is an astonishing work of art, in which spirit and matter have merged. No ancient statue is a more vivid reminder that Nike also was the goddess of spiritual victory—that victory over one's own ego that leads to wisdom.

Athena Being Born from the Head of Zeus
(black-figure amphora). Attic, 5th century B.C.E.
Ceramic, height: 15 in. (38 cm). Musée du Louvre, Paris.

Athena. Greece, 340–330 B.C.E.
Bronze. National Archaeological Museum, Athens.

Athena with Her Serpent. Greece, 5th century B.C.E.
Carnelian. British Museum, London.

Athena Parthenos with Nike, Serpent, and Shield. Antique copy of the Parthenon statue by Phidias, 5th century B.C.E. Marble. National Archaeological Museum, Athens.

Nike (Victory) (from the balustrade surrounding the Temple of Athena Nike). Greece, c. 410–407 B.C.E. Marble, height: 42 in. (106.3 cm). Acropolis Museum, Athens.

Nike ("Winged Victory of Samothrace"). Greece, c. 190 B.C.E.
Marble and limestone, height: 129⅛ in. (328 cm).
Musée du Louvre, Paris.

GODDESSES OF KNOWLEDGE
AND WISDOM

It is one thing to have knowledge. It is another to have wisdom. The traditional world has goddesses for both. Just as there are goddesses for every aspect of the natural world, so there are goddesses for every kind of learning. Most numerous are patron deities for all the handicrafts: from cooking, spinning, weaving, and pottery to the making of bronze, iron, and gold. Almost as plentiful are patron deities of music, dance, and the visual arts. No lessons were more important than those learned during the initiation rites that transformed an adolescent into an adult member of the tribe or city-state. This teaching was usually done by a shaman or shamaness in the tribal world and by semishamanic priests and priestesses in Bronze Age civilizations, all in the name of the highest deities.

In a few cultures there is one deity who patronizes all art and knowledge, or a small group of deities such as the Muses (see pages 234–35). In India she is Sarasvati (page 236), who was born of Brahma after he turned into an Androgyne. The fertile goddess of rivers, who flew on a swan (symbol of transcendent reality), Sarasvati grew more complex as the Aryans became agricultural and literate. She invented all the arts, including speaking, singing, writing (so the sacred songs could be recorded), and shamanic healing. She patronizes all forms of creativity and intellectual work, including the quest for wisdom. In the words of David Kinsley, author of *Hindu Goddesses* (1986), she is the "ever-flowing stream of celestial grace which purifies . . . the earth." The Hindu goddess who embodies the energy of wisdom is Kundalini, whose symbolic form is the double serpent.

Tara, the star goddess of Tibet (pages 241–43), also encourages every way of knowing, particularly the spiritual knowing that leads to that mastery of self called enlightenment or grace. She also is the essence of compassion for all living beings. In China, Kuan-Yin (like Tara and Sarasvati) is the personification of boundless, unconditional love (pages 238–40). How to be at one with her essence is the purpose of the esoteric teachings of all the wisdom paths. Having started as a Taoist Mother Goddess, she then was assimilated by the Buddhists. She has a central place in virtually all the traditional homes of China and Japan, where her name is Kannon. It is said that she once lived on earth until she rose to heaven on a rainbow. Like all bodhisattvas, after she attained enlightenment, following many lifetimes, she chose to retain human form so she could respond to every prayer until all beings were liberated from themselves and lived at peace with one another.

In the Old Testament, God's cocreator is a female divinity named Hokhma, which means "wisdom." Those within the Judeo-Christian tradition who say "God alone created the universe" have not read some parts of the Old Testament. Hokhma is said to have been there "from the beginning" of God's creation. In Proverbs (8:22–29) we read that she was there before the beginning of earth and the heavens, when God "drew out a circle on the face of the deep." Moreover, it was the shadow of Hokhma that stilled the primal waters, as she acted in partnership with God during the process of creation. She also gave consciousness to humanity. In Proverbs (4:7–8), we are told that "Wisdom is the principal thing; therefore, get wisdom. . . . Exalt her . . . embrace her."

All-loving wisdom also was central to what Athena stood for as the Athenian goddess of wisdom. In Greek Christianity, Athena became Sophia—"Divine Wisdom." In her earliest manifestations, Athena's totemic allies were the owl of wisdom and the double serpent of nonduality. These attributes tended to be neglected as the Athenians changed from a goddess-oriented society of farmers to a god-oriented society of warriors and merchants, but they never entirely disappeared from the sacred symbolism by which she is represented.

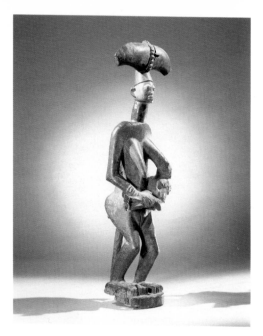

Mother and Child (Oya, Mate of Schango). Yoruba tribe, Nigeria, c. 19th century. Wood with paint, height: 28½ in. (72.4 cm). The Metropolitan Museum of Art, New York; The Michael C. Rockefeller Memorial Collection, Bequest of Nelson A. Rockefeller, 1979.

Oromila, Goddess of Divine Knowledge.
Bini tribe, Benin City, Nigeria, c. 19th century.
Ivory. British Museum, London.

Goddess Who Kills Witches, and Her Mate (helmet masks).
Senufo tribe, Ivory Coast, c. 19th century. Wood.
Rietberg Museum, Zurich.

Inkosazana(?), Goddess of Divine Knowledge.
Zulu tribe, South Africa, 20th century(?). Wood.
Musée de l'Homme, Paris.

Athena, Goddess of Wisdom (the goddess in a gown
of living snakes). Greece, 6th century B.C.E.(?).
Bronze. National Archaeological Museum, Athens.

Gustav Klimt (1862–1914). *Pallas Athena*, 1898.
Oil on canvas, 29⅝ x 29⅝ in. (75 x 75 cm). Historisches
Museum der Stadt Wien, Vienna.

The Achilles Painter (n.d.). *Muse on Mount Helikon.*
Attic, c. 445 B.C.E. Ceramic, height: 14½ in. (36.7 cm).
Staatliche Antikensammlungen, Munich.

Sarcophagus of the Muses. Roman, c. 150-60.
Marble, 23⅝ x 81⅛ in. (60 x 206 cm).
Musée du Louvre, Paris.

Sarasvati. India, c. 1860. Watercolor.
The Victoria and Albert Museum, London.

Isis Guiding the Queen-Goddess Nofretari
(from Nofretari's tomb at Abu Simbel).
Egypt, c. 1300 B.C.E.

Horse-Headed Bodhisattva of Compassion (Batō-Kannon).
Japan, 11th century. Ink, pigments,
and gold on silk, height: 65¾ in. (166 cm).
Museum of Fine Arts, Boston; Fenollosa-Weld Collection.

SENGAI (1751–1837). *Kannon and Sutra* (detail), 1823.
Ink on silk, 35⅝ x 15⅜ in. (90.1 x 38.9 cm).
Seattle Art Museum; Gift of Harold Rogers.

Kuan-Yin, Seated on the Lotus Throne of Wisdom.
China, 20th century. Porcelain.
Art Information Center, Northbank, California.

Tara, with the Lotus of Wisdom. Nepal, 16th century. Copper, gilt, semiprecious stones, and paint, height (without stand): 20¼ in. (51.2 cm). The Metropolitan Museum of Art, New York; Purchase, 1966, Louis V. Bell Fund.

White Tara. Nepal, 15th century. Gilt bronze and precious stones, 21½ x 17 x 12½ in. (54.6 x 43.2 x 31.8 cm). Asian Art Museum of San Francisco; Avery Brundage Collection.

MARIANNA RYDVALD (b. 1944). *Green Tara in the Jungle*
(detail), 1992. Oil on canvas, 60 x 72 in. (151 x 182 cm).
Collection of the artist.

THE SPIRIT OF THE GODDESS
IN MODERN ART

Except in rural regions, where some still pray to Mother Earth for fertility, virtually all citizens of Western civilization stopped worshiping goddesses many centuries ago. Some say Mary is the goddess of Christianity. The mother of Jesus certainly is a saint and is regarded as the Queen of Heaven by many; however, officially she is a reflection of God and not divine herself. The idea of goddesses has continued into secular modern society but usually as no more than a lightweight metaphor for Venus—often merely an excuse for rendering ladies nude. In an unbelieving world, the closest things to goddesses are allegorical images of Freedom, Democracy, and Knowledge in nineteenth-century art. Personifications of Liberty appear on coins and as the well-known statue in New York Harbor; the Great Seal of the State of California features Minerva. Millions of people carry images of Liberty or Minerva in their pockets and purses every day, but few look at these icons and realize that they are descendants of the goddess of wisdom and the goddess of victory.

The definition of the word *goddess* has been progressively diluted in the modern era. By the nineteenth century the word had started to have a new, secular meaning:

not a female who is divine in the original sense but any woman who is particularly beautiful. The distinction started to blur between the beauty of holiness and the holiness of beauty. Hollywood has made much of this modern definition. Today, the word *goddess* is used more often in association with movie stars than in any other context. Millions of people who have never seen a traditional goddess image have derived their idea of what a "real goddess" must look like from Hollywood films. Every decade sees more movies that feature various "goddess" roles, from the Stone Age "daughter of the gods," usually bathing naked, to high priestesses of the biblical–Bronze Age type, usually surrounded by giant statues of deities, large snakes, and the sensuous aura of Babylonian decadence. The most popular goddess role of all has been Cleopatra, who in real life was both the queen of Egypt and a goddess worshiped by the ancient Egyptians. In the modern world, Cleopatra's face and form have been that of Theda Bara (page 250), Vivien Leigh, and especially Elizabeth Taylor (page 251), in dramatic productions as elaborate and costly as the original ceremonies honoring the Great Goddess some two thousand years ago.

At the end of the nineteenth century the Symbolist artists attempted to revive meaningful images of goddesses (pages 193, 252), but only a limited number of people were interested. In the first half of this century the most important artists to continue the Symbolists' interest in the deeper meaning of goddess mythology were the Surrealists (pages 256–57) and the Abstract Expressionists. From Max Ernst to Jackson Pollock, these artists were attempting to do what shamanic art has always done—to reveal the radiance of the transcendent shining through all matter, to suggest the luminous goddess glowing under her veils. Goddess-oriented modernists such as Jean Arp (page 158), Paul Klee (page 195), and Joan Miró (page 253), for example, articulated fresh visions of the primordial Androgyne, having been inspired by Stone Age art. New conceptions of the goddess as the primal female in twentieth-century art became increasingly common with the advent of the women's movement, the goddess movement, and postmodernism in the 1960s and '70s. Since then, goddess images by men and women have become an important part of contemporary art. Among the most widely published works are those by Judy Chicago (page 264), Audrey Flack (pages 77, 212), Niki de Saint Phalle (page 197), and Jerry N. Uelsmann (pages 262–63).

During the same decades, ecology-minded scientists returned to goddess imagery and developed the "Gaia hypothesis" as a way of comprehending the earth as a single organism. Perhaps the most historically important new images of the late twentieth century are NASA's photographs of the earth from space (page 249). For the first time, the children of Gaia, Mother Earth, have been able to see her as a single luminous totality, undivided by political boundaries. If the Great Goddess is to return as a central reality in the mythology of the twenty-first century, this photographic image may well be the form in which she is seen most often. She will not be a local, tribal, or national goddess but a global goddess sacred to all the people of our planet.

View of Earth from Apollo 17, 1972.

Theda Bara as Cleopatra, 1917.

Elizabeth Taylor as Cleopatra, 1963.

FRANTISEK KUPKA (1871–1957). *The Lotus Soul* (detail), 1898.
Watercolor. Narodni Galerie, Prague.

JOAN MIRÓ (1893–1983). *Dawn Perfumed by a Shower of Gold,* 1954. Watercolor and plaster on composition board, 42½ x 21⅝ in. (108 x 54.9 cm). San Francisco Museum of Modern Art; Gift of Wilbur D. May.

PIERRE-AUGUSTE RENOIR (1841-1919). *The Judgment of Paris,*
c. 1915. Oil on canvas, 31 x 40 in. (80 x 101 cm).
Hiroshima Museum of Art, Hiroshima, Japan.

ARISTIDE MAILLOL (1861–1944). *Torso of L'Ile de France*, 1921.
Bronze, 30 x 14 x 22¼ in. (76.2 x 35.6 x 56.5 cm).
Fine Arts Museums of San Francisco;
Mildred Anna Williams Collection.

SALVADOR DALÍ (1904–1989). *Shirley Temple, the Youngest Monster Sacred to the Cinema of Her Time (The Sphinx)*, 1939. Gouache, pastel, and collage on board, 29⅝ x 39⅛ in. (75 x 100 cm). Museum Boymans-van Beuningen, Rotterdam, the Netherlands.

MAX ERNST (1891–1976). *The Robing of the Bride*, 1939–40.
Oil on canvas. Peggy Guggenheim Collection, Venice.

257

HENRY MOORE (1898–1986). *Reclining Figure*, 1938.
Bronze. Tate Gallery, London.

Barbara Hepworth (1903–1975). *Curved Form (Anima)*, 1959. Bronze, 25½ x 27¾ x 15 in. (64.8 x 70.5 x 38 cm). Everson Museum of Art, Syracuse, New York.

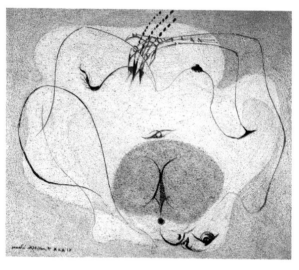

ANDRÉ MASSON (1896–1987). *The Earth,* 1939.
Sand and oil on wood.
Musée National d'Art Moderne, Paris.

JAMES PIERCE (b. 1930). *Earthwoman,* 1976-77.
Earth, 5 x 30 x 15 ft. (1.5 x 9.1 x 4.5 m).
Pratt Farm, Maine.

JERRY N. UELSMANN (b. 1934). *Untitled*, 1994.
Gelatin silver print. Collection of the artist.

JERRY N. UELSMANN (b. 1934). *Untitled*, 1981.
Gelatin silver print. Collection of the artist.

JUDY CHICAGO (b. 1939). *The Birth Project: Earth Birth,* 1983.
Airbrush and quilting, 63 x 135 in. (159.3 x 341.5 cm).
Quilted by Jacqueline Moore. Collection of the artist.

IRENE YOUNG (n.d.). *Snake Goddess at Knossos,* 1989.
Photocollage. Collection of the artist.

CAROLEE SCHNEEMANN (b. 1939). *Eye Body*, 1963.
Performance photo. Collection of the artist.

CHERI GAULKE (b. 1954). Video production still
from *Revelations of the Flesh*, 1985.
Performance with Susan Maberry.

Sha Sha Higby (n.d.). *Pineapple Sunset,* 1990.
Collection of the artist.

BARBARA KASTEN (n.d.). *Tanagra Goddess IX,* 1995.
Cibachrome print, 30 x 20 in. (76 x 50.6 cm).
Yancey Richardson Gallery, New York.

ANN McCoy (b. 1946). *Altar II*, 1989.
Cast bronze and lead over wood, 54 x 28 x 6 in.
(136.6 x 70.8 x 15.2 cm). Courtesy of the artist.

Cast of Characters

Ala Ibo Mother Goddess in Nigeria.

Amaterasu Japanese Great Goddess, supreme deity of the sun, the family, and wisdom. Chief deity of the Shinto tradition. Her symbol is the rising sun, which appears on the Japanese flag.

Aphrodite/Venus Greek/Roman goddess of love. To philosophers she has two primary aspects: transcendental love (Urania) and common lust (Porne).

Artemis/Diana Greek/Roman virgin goddess of the moon, the animals, and the woods. Twin of the sun god and beloved guardian spirit of childbirth in animals and humans. Quite possibly of Minoan origin.

Ashtoreth (Asherah) Canaanite goddess of fertility, often described in the Old Testament; related to Ishtar. She holds a lotus in one hand and a pair of serpents in the other; often she is nude. Related to Astarte and Ishtar.

Astarte ("Queen of Heaven") Great Goddess of the Phoenicians and Assyrians. Related to Ishtar and Ashtoreth.

Athena/Minerva Greek/Roman goddess of wisdom and war, quite possibly of Minoan origin. Virgin daughter of Zeus. Protector of Athens; the Parthenon is her shrine.

Bast Egyptian goddess of childbirth, health, healing, and war. She has the head either of a cat (lunar) or a lion (solar). 271

Brigid (Briganta, Bride; "Bright One") Early Christian saint who previously was a powerful Celtic goddess of healing in Ireland, Scotland, England, and France. "Baptized" by Saint Patrick.

Britomartis ("Sweet Maiden") Minoan moon goddess, who seems to embody the female essence of nature. Possibly the name of the Great Goddess of life, death, and rebirth in Minoan Crete. Her power animal was the snake.

Ceres *See* Demeter.

Coatlicue Aztec Great Goddess of life, death, and rebirth. Androgynous mother of Quetzalcoatl. She wears a skirt of serpents and a necklace of skulls; her head is a double serpent or a skull. She is the earth and the pyramid.

Cybele Near Eastern Great Goddess from Phrygia who came to Rome. Sacred Marriage partner of Attis, her offspring. Usually shown with lions, but her first embodiment was a stone. She is the earth and the mother of all.

Demeter/Ceres Greek/Roman goddess, personifying the fertility of the fields. Her daughter (Demeter's virginal aspect) is Persephone/Proserpine, who personifies the crop that is reborn from the earth each spring. Demeter and Persephone together embody the forces of eternal rebirth.

Diana *See* Artemis.

Durga Hindu Great Goddess of life and death, love and justice. Said to be the primal manifestation of universal energy and stronger than any of the gods who emanate from her (in the male-oriented versions of the myth, she emanates from them). Usually portrayed as a warrior who defeats evil with female helpers such as Kali, who is often considered her demonic offspring. She also grants ultimate liberation from suffering by guiding the faithful to enlightenment.

Europa Minoan moon goddess, who was abducted to Europe by Zeus personified as a bull. The word *Europe* comes from her name.

Flora Roman goddess of flowers and the flowering of all nature. The word *flower* comes from her name.

Frig (Frigg, Frigga; "Beloved") Great Goddess of Scandinavians and North Teutons, who is thought of as wisdom, healing, virgin, mother, and the energy of rebirth. Probably Freya (Freyja) was her name when she was thought of as the goddess of sex, war, and death. Her totems are falcons and hawks. Wife of Odin (Woden). The word *Friday* comes from her name.

Gaia (Gaea, Ge) Greek Great Goddess, who is the earth. Androgynous creator of time (Chronos), space (Uranus), and all of humanity's ancestors.

Ganga Hindu goddess of rivers and healing. Half of her is the Milky Way; half of her is the sacred river the Ganges. She also provides health, wealth, and happiness.

Gorgons Three Greek sisters from "beyond the sea" with horrid faces and serpents for hair. Their meaning is uncertain, but likely they were originally triple goddesses of death and rebirth. Athena took over the serpentine power of the one mortal sister, Medusa.

Harmonia ("Harmony") Greek goddess of healing, knowledge, and creativity. Daughter of Aphrodite (love) and Ares (war), she guides humanity in balancing these two forces.

Hathor Egyptian Great Goddess of life, death, and rebirth. Mother of Egypt; mother and daughter of the sun god. Isis assumed many of her features. Usually embodied as a cow but also seen as a lion, a tree, or a woman. Guardian of all women and female animals. A patron of sensuous pleasures; the Greeks compared her to Aphrodite.

Hera Greek Great Goddess. Primordial androgynous creator, known as the cow-eyed Queen of Heaven. Later the unhappy wife of Zeus. (The parallel Roman goddess is Juno, wife of Jupiter.) The force of life, death, and rebirth, she is patron of all women.

Hokhma (Hokhmah; "Wisdom") Jewish name for God's partner in the creation myth told in Proverbs. Personification of wisdom.

Hygeia ("Health") Greek goddess of health and healing. Daughter of Asklepios and Epione.

Inanna (Queen of Heaven) Sumerian Great Goddess and hence primary goddess of the world's first known civilization. She later became known in Mesopotamia as Ishtar. Her consorts continuously die and are continuously reborn.

Iris (Messenger of Light) Greek goddess who, as the rainbow, brings the healing power of the Mother Goddess from the sky to earth. She carries the caduceus and sleeps under Hera's bed (or throne).

Ishtar ("Light-Giving") Mesopotamian Great Goddess of life, death, and rebirth. Of Semitic origin, she was worshiped throughout the Assyro-Babylonian world as the deity of love, fertility, healing, and war. She has different names in many nations. Her offspring-consort was a vegetation god who died and was reborn each year. Related to Ashtoreth and Astarte.

Isis Egyptian Great Goddess of life, death, and rebirth. Daughter of earth and sky; mother of Horus, the falcon god. Wife of her brother Osiris, the god-king of vegetation and eternal life. She gave life after death to her husband. The eternal salvation that she could bestow was originally (in the Bronze Age) only for the god-king but gradually, as the cult became democratic in the Iron Age, it became available to all humans.

Juno *See* Hera.

Kali Hindu Great Goddess of life, death, and rebirth. Widely pictured as "Black Mother Time." Kali sometimes has a male consort, but he is always subordinate. She kills him, just as she kills everything else in the world to which she gave birth. Her grim images, in which she is often drinking blood, are among the most frightening in the history of art. *See* Durga.

Ki (Ninki; "Earth") Sumerian earth goddess. Her original mythic form seems to have been in union with An, the sky god. Her symbol was probably the double serpent.

Kuan-Yin/Kannon Far Eastern goddess. Originally a Taoist Mother Goddess, she was assimilated by the Buddhists as a deity of infinite love and boundless compassion. She is revered throughout China and Japan, usually in the form of a white figure with flowing robes and sometimes accompanied by her power creature, the dragon—symbol of universal energy manifesting in space and time.

Kundalini Tantric Hindu goddess who dwells coiled at the base of the spine as a snake but can rise up through the chakras as one's psychic energy moves toward enlightenment. Her symbol, a double serpent, is at least as old as the Bronze Age and may date back to the Stone Age. She symbolizes primal being.

Ma-Ku (Ma-Gu) Chinese goddess of springtime, health, and healing.

Minerva Etruscan/Roman goddess of wisdom and knowledge. Her name derives from the word for mind. *See* Athena, from whom she may well have developed.

Muses Greek goddesses (sometimes three but usually nine) of art and inspiration. Daughters of Mnemosyne ("Memory").

Mut Egyptian Mother Goddess, originally from Nubia. An androgynous world mother and goddess of magic, healing, and immortality. Many of her functions were taken over by Isis, Hathor, et al., during the Bronze Age. Usually portrayed as a vulture.

Neith (Net) Egyptian cow goddess, mother of Ra (the sun god) and of all humans. Her priests and priestesses were healers. She was patron of all the crafts.

Nephthys (Nebthet) Egyptian goddess, sister of Isis and her exact opposite. The realm of Isis is life and rebirth; the realm of Nephthys is death and the tomb.

Nike/Victoria Greek/Roman winged goddess of military and spiritual victory.

Nommo (Nummo) African goddess-god of the Dogon in Mali. Androgynous deity of creation, tribes, families, and waters.

Nowa African goddess of the Sande and Yassi shamanesses of the Mende and related tribes in Sierra Leone and Liberia.

Nut Egyptian sky goddess and mother of the sun god, Ra, to whom she gives birth each morning and whom she swallows each night. Wife of her brother, the earth god, Geb; mother of Isis and Osiris.

Nu-Wa (Nu-Kua, Nügua) Chinese Great Goddess, who is the androgynous creator of humans, from yellow clay. She and her male aspect have the bodies of serpents and usually are seen intertwined, forming the primal image of the double serpent. Sometimes seen as a rainbow dragon or as a woman. She also tamed the animals and created the first civilization, which probably was matristic.

Oshun Yoruba river goddess of fertility and healing in Nigeria. Mate of Shango. Migrated to Central and South America.

Pali Kongju Tribal Korean goddess of healing. Patron of male and female shamans.

Parvati ("She of the Mountains") Hindu Great Goddess of life, death, and rebirth. Androgynous creator and the female half of the Great God Shiva when he is the Androgyne. Daughter of Himavati (divine personification of the Himalayas) and Mena ("Mind"); mother (without male participation) of Ganesha (the elephant god of good fortune). Benevolent aspect of Kali. Commonly regarded as the ideal wife and patron of womanhood.

Pasiphaë ("She Who Shines for All") Minoan goddess. Daughter of the sun and moon. In her human form she was the queen-priestess of Crete who, as the cow goddess, mated with the bull god in a shamanic Sacred Marriage. The legendary result of this union was the Minotaur.

Persephone/Proserpine ("Maiden") Greek/Roman goddess of agricultural and spiritual rebirth. Wife of Zeus's brother Hades. She is protected by the double serpent. *See* Demeter.

Proserpine *See* Persephone.

Radha ("Beloved One") Hindu goddess of sexuality who, as a consort of Vishnu, represents the metaphysical longing of every soul for union with the divine. Her priestesses today are still naked; her rituals are secret.

Sarah ("Princess") Hebrew matriarch and possibly a Chaldean priestess. Wife and sister of Abraham. Many scholars think she actually was a goddess of fertility and healing whose divinity was veiled in the Old Testament.

Sarasvati ("Flowering One") Originally a Hindu goddess of rivers and fertility, she became the goddess of knowledge and wisdom as well as of the arts.

Sekhmet ("Powerful") Egyptian goddess of war, whose totem creatures are the lion and the cat.

Selket Egyptian goddess, guardian of the dead and of marriage. Her totem creature is the scorpion.

Shakti ("Energy") Aspect of the Hindu deity who in his male manifestation represents the transcendent stillness of the eternal, while she is the energy that brings his divine presence into the material world. Sometimes called Durga, Kali, or Parvati.

Shekhinah ("Indwelling") Jewish name for the female aspect of God. Regarded by some as a goddess. Esoterically, she is perceived as the emanation of God who dwells within every individual.

Sita ("Furrow") Hindu goddess and human incarnation of Lakshmi, goddess of abundance, who came to the earth to destroy an evil king and marry Vishnu in the form of Rama. Like Parvati, she is regarded as the ideal devoted wife.

Spider-Woman Native American (Hopi, Navajo, et al.) goddess of creation.

Tara ("Star") Hindu, Jain, and Tibetan Buddhist goddess who helps all humans to extinguish desire. As Green Tara, she can be demonic. As White Tara, she peacefully guides meditators beyond fear to eternity.

Taranga Polynesian goddess of vegetation, initiation, life, and death. Mother of Maui, who brought knowledge of agriculture to the Polynesian people.

Tauret Egyptian goddess of childbirth, embodied as a hippopotamus.

Tonantzin (Tonantsi; "Revered Mother")/Chicomecoatl ("Serpent") Androgynous Aztec goddess of the harvest, especially maize. She is the "ancestor" of the Virgin of Guadalupe.

Venus *See* Aphrodite.

Index of Illustrations

282

283

285

Photography Credits

The photographers and the sources of photographic material other than those indicated in the captions are as follows (numerals refer to page numbers, unless otherwise indicated).

© 1997 Artists Rights Society (ARS), New York/ADAGP, Paris: 253; Art Resource, New York: 236; Art Resource, New York and © 1997 Artists Rights Society (ARS), New York/VG Bild-Kunst, Bonn: 158; Asia Society, New York: 114 (photo: Lynton Gardiner), 115 (photo: Lynton Gardiner), 224 (photo: Mr. Wakisaka); Borromeo, Milan/Art Resource, New York: 88, 89, 164; Bridgeman Art Library, London: 217; © Bibliothèque de l'Assemblée Nationale, Paris: 171 (photo: Larousse); © Alan Bowness, Hepworth Estate: 259 (photo: Hugh Tifft); © British Museum, London: 66 (registration no. 1886-314), 85, 108 (registration no. 1910-441), 126, 170 (registration no. 1896.2-2.1), 202 (registration no. 1898.10-25.1), 203 (registration no. 1944.Af4.12), 204 (registration no. 1949.Af46.410), 205 (registration no. 1901.7-22.1), 220, 229 (registration no. 1949.Af46.169); Cameraphoto, Venice/Art Resource, New York: © 1997 and Artists Rights Society (ARS), New York/ADAGP, Paris: 257; Canadian Museum of Civilization, Hull: 103 (image number s88-2200); © 1997 Demart Pro Arte®, Geneva/Artists Rights Society (ARS), New York: 256;

Field Museum, Chicago: 119 (neg. #A110674C; photo: Ron Testa), 127 (neg. #A11069C, photo: Ron Testa), 167 (neg. #A113120C, photo: John Weinstein), 172 (neg. # A109444C, photo: Ron Testa); Werner Forman/Art Resource, New York: 68, 71, 74; Fox Films, courtesy Kobal: 250; Giraudon/Art Resource, New York: 6, 51, 56, 60, 152, 192, 193; Giraudon/Art Resource, New York, © 1997 and Artists Rights Society (ARS), New York/ADAGP, Paris: 260; Courtesy Lanier Graham: 163, 240, 268; Max Hirmer, Hirmer Verlag, Munich: 237; Hubert Josse/Abbeville Press: 46, 49, 54, 84, 100, 116, 118, 128, 130, 150, 151, 154, 176, 184, 186, 187, 223, 235; Paidma Kaimal/Abbeville Press: 180; Georgios Katsagelos/Abbeville Press: 52, 110, 148, 155, 156, 179, 220, 232; Erich Lessing/Art Resource, New York: 15, 76, 78–79, 188, 210, 213, 218, 232; Paul Macapia: 239; Michele Maier: 24; © Manchester City Art Galleries: 153; Courtesy Louis K. Meisel Gallery, New York: 77 (photo: Steven Lopez); Metropolitan Museum of Art, New York: 228 (1979.206.10, photo: Justin Kerr); Photo courtesy Robert Miller Gallery: 141; © Priya Mookerjee: 65; Courtesy D. C. Moore Gallery, New York: 162; Musée d'Aquitaine, Bordeaux: 38; © Musée de l'Homme, Paris: 41 (photo: A. Marshack), 45 (photo: B. Hatala), 70, 80, 90 (photo: D. Destable & Lemzaaouda), 231 (photo: D. Destable & Lemzaaouda); Museo Nazionale Ro-

mano, All Rights Reserved: 157; © 1995 Museum Associates, Los Angeles County Museum of Art: 62, 63; Photo © 1985 Museum of Fine Arts, Boston: 1, 21, 34, 53, 124, 133, 181, 228, 244; Photo © 1996 The Museum of Modern Art, New York: 138; Museum of Navajo Ceremonial Art, Santa Fe: 174 (photo: Roderick Hook); Nimatallah/Art Resource, New York: 2, 64, 111, 112, 146–47, 159, 161, 214, 218, 222; Takashi Okamura/Abbeville Press: 10; James Pierce: 261; Photo © RMN: 43 (photo: Gerard Blot); 166; Scala/Art Resource, New York: 44, 48, 50, 102, 113, 132, 134, 135, 136, 142, 160, 169, 182, 184, 187, 189; Schalkwijk/Art Resource, New York: 117; © 1995 Sotheby's, Inc.: 136; Studio Koppermann, München: 234; Tate Gallery, London/Art Resource, New York, reproduced by permission of the Henry Moore Foundation: 258; Courtesy Thames and Hudson, Ltd., London: 26; 20th Century Fox, courtesy Kobal: 251; University of Pennsylvania Museum, Philadelphia: 91 (neg. #29-12-97), 123 (neg. #57-18-1), 198 (neg. #37-22-279); Vancouver Museum: 75 (cat. #AA1177); Victoria and Albert Museum, London/Art Resource, New York: 182; © 1996 Andy Warhol Foundation for the Visual Arts/ars, New York: 191; © Foto Wettstein & Kauf, Museum Rietberg, Zurich: 230; Photo © 1996 Whitney Museum of American Art, New York, and © 1997 Artists Rights Society (ARS), New York/ADAGP, Paris: 197.

286

Editor: Nancy Grubb
Designer: Kevin Callahan
Production Editor: Jeffrey Golick
Picture Editors: Naomi Ben-Shahar and Alysia Kaplan
Production Manager: Stacy Rockwood

First edition
10 9 8 7 6 5 4 3 2 1

Library of Congress Cataloging-in-Publication Data
Graham, F. Lanier.
    Goddesses / Lanier Graham.
        p. cm.
    "A tiny folio."
    Includes indexes.
    ISBN 0-7892-0269-7
    1. Goddesses.   2. Goddess religion.   I. Title.
BL325.F4G73   1997
291.2'114—dc21   96-47142

SELECTED TINY FOLIOS™ FROM ABBEVILLE PRESS

- American Impressionism 1-55859-801-4 • $11.95
- Angels 0-7892-0025-2 • $11.95
- The Art of Tarot 0-7892-0016-3 • $11.95
- The Great Book of French Impressionism 1-55859-336-5 • $11.95
- Japanese Prints: The Art Institute of Chicago 1-55859-803-0 • $11.95
- Treasures of British Art: Tate Gallery 1-55859-772-7 • $11.95
- Treasures of Folk Art 1-55859-560-0 • $11.95
- Treasures of Impressionism and Post-Impressionism: National Gallery of Art 1-55859-561-9 • $11.95
- Treasures of the Louvre 1-55859-477-9 • $11.95
- Treasures of the Musée d'Orsay 1-55859-783-2 • $11.95
- Treasures of the Musée Picasso 1-55859-836-7 • $11.95
- Treasures of the National Museum of the American Indian 0-7892-0105-4 • $11.95
- Treasures of 19th- and 20th-Century Painting: The Art Institute of Chicago 1-55859-603-8 • $11.95
- Treasures of the Prado 1-55859-558-9 • $11.95
- Treasures of the Uffizi 1-55859-559-7 • $11.95
- Women Artists: The National Museum of Women in the Arts 1-55859-890-1 • $11.95